SPITFIRE
THE MAKINGS OF A REVOLUTIONARY

A True Life Story

By

Ashanti A. A. Ali

© 2019 Califa Media Publishing™

A Moorish Guide Publishing Company
MOORISH RELIGIOUS & CULTURAL INSTITUTE, INC.
Lafayette, Indiana

SpitFire
The Makings of a Revolutionary
A True Life Story

Written By
Ashanti A. A. Ali

© 2019
Califa Media Publishing
A Moorish Guide Publishing Company
MOORISH RELIGIOUS & CULTURAL INSTITUTE, INC.
Lafayette, Indiana

Library of Congress Control Number: 2019944353 [978-1096449027]
ISBN-13: 978-1-952828-07-2

All Rights Reserved. Without Prejudice. No Part Of This Book May Be Reproduced Or Transmitted In Any Form By Any Means, Electronic, Photocopying, Mechanical, Recording, Information Storage Or Retrieval System Unless For The Liberation Of Minds And Gaining Knowledge Of Self.

Cover design and original art
by Sis. T. Najee-Ullah El

CONTENTS

AUTHOR'S NOTE	I
CHAPTER 1	1
CAN'T EVEN DO WRONG RIGHT	
CHAPTER 2	4
STRUCK BY LIGHTENING	
CHAPTER 3	8
MISSISSIPPI	
(PLAY-N-DIRTY POOL)	
CHAPTER 4	16
BACK ON THE BLOCK	
(PIMPS AND PUNKS)	
CHAPTER 5	24
LOOK + LISTEN = LEARN	
CHAPTER 6	39
PRISON	
CHAPTER 7	47
DECLARATION	
(THE WORLD'S 1ST COMMUNIST MUSLIM SOCIALIST)	
CHAPTER 8	73
THE DEVIL TIP-TOED INTO HEAVEN WHILE GOD SLEPT	
CHAPTER 9	116
CLOSING ARGUMENTS	
DEDICATION	151

Author's Note

```
                         U.S. CONSTITUTION


                           AMENDMENT 1


     Congress shall make no law respecting establishment of
religion, or prohibiting the free exercise thereof; or
abridging the freedom of speech, or the press; or the right
of the people peaceably to assemble, and petition the
government for a redress of grievence.




                  [The amendments protect individuals
                   from various unjust acts of the
                   government. The first 10 amendments,
                   known as the Bill of Rights, were
                   proposed on September 25, 1789. They
                   were ratified (approved) on December
                   15, 1791].




               _____


     RE:            SPITFIRE!
                    THE MAKINGS OF A REVOLUTIONARY
                    THE TRUE LIFE STORY OF ASHANTI ALI,


All chapter-content is soley the work by the author, Ashanti Ali,
inwhich he and he alone shall be fully responsible for this work,
and, as such, the Publisher is not in any way, shape or form, to
be viewed as responsible, nor should the publisher of this work,
SPITFIRE, in the unforseeable future, " libel concern surface."
be deemed responsible in any court of law, now and future.



                                        Ashanti Ali
                                           -x-
                                        Michael Jackson

                                        xMichael Jackson
                                        right thumb print
```

i

Chapter 1
Can't Even Do Wrong Right

"Who are you, I am asked
If I give A name
It only tells what I am called
It still does not say
Who nor what I am.

To the oppressed, I am the angel of deliverance
To the oppressor I am the angel of destruction
So who I am
Depends on who you are."

    (Comrade)

    (Sheik Nuh Abdul'Qayyum)

    X

    (Albert Nuh Washington)

    Folsom 8/22/1975

July 12, 1977, my celly would be murdered right before my eyes in San Quentin's infamous East Block. I watch as his memory was being etched into the grey matter in my cranium forever. Stabbed 27 times, and kicked under the rail, he fell from the fourth tier. I've never been the same.

The Muslim brotherhood would immediately group-up, engage in perhaps a one-minute discussion, and become mobile. They tracked down the leaders of the American Nazi Socialist (ANS), cornered them, and took them out, Johnny on the spot. The Muslims didn't stop there: Brother Secretary, who himself had just come down off the row, set his sights on the Warden who had come out because of the enormous amount of gunshots and sheer roars which tend to vibrate throughout the Q. **The whites had effected a simultaneous move on the Blacks all over San Quentin.**

Brother Secretary (x-Milton) took off on the Warden himself and straight downed him right there on the spot. Left him lying there and walked back to the three columns of Muslims. At that juncture, Muslims were some 154 deep on the mainline in Quentin. Organized to the tee, folks knew to give them a wide berth indeed.

The Nazis, in posthaste, mistook my celly, Charles Captain, for me. A true case of mistaken identity for real and for sure. The price tag was enormous. San Quentin would be locked down for more than a year. A war was brewing. I was young, fresh to the line, and inexperienced in how they get down in prison minus the hearsay bequeathed unto me in the county jail. But, the one thing I wasn't was a coward.

I was fortunate enough to have been in the company of true to form revolutionaries prior to my capture. I was well drilled in numerous forms of combat, notwithstanding I am an Army veteran. I had escaped being so-called executed on death row only to descend into an environment of puritanical racism. I entertained fish lines[1] galore each day, every day, all day from the radical "BDF" there in East Block with me, telling me I "had to take a military course of action" for what the "white boys" did to my celly. Bottom line.

I let it be known in no uncertain terms: oh, it's going down on sight. I actually would stab an individual, Peacock—he had a giant peacock tatted on his back and that's exactly where I left my knife. I left it stuck in a

---

[1] Written message soliciting sexual intercourse. http://urbandictionary.com.

protruding from his back. It should be known that it was much more to all this targeting than met the eye. And, perhaps it would be a wise man's move to freeze, back up, and highlight just what ushered all this madness in.

To engage such, I must redirect focus back to my life prior to being captured, for it has a direct tie to what took place here in prison. My name and adventures, so to speak, had preceded me and I was well known in the California prison system long before I arrived. Here now, I shall attempt to contrast it all.

There exist those who believe I am here for some specific reason or another. This, primarily, is because of some of the things I have experienced. One situation occurred when I was only five years old. It took place on the streets of west Oakland. This memory brings to mind the words of the Most Honorable Elijah Muhammad: EVERYTHING HAPPENS ON TIME, IN TIME, ALL THE TIME AND NOTHING HAPPENS OUT OF TIME. (HEM, 1964).

I often reflect here in my cell how, as a youth, our school took our sociology class on a tour of both Alcatraz and San Quentin. Never in my wildest dreams did I ever think that someday, I would be a resident. The tour had the same effect on me that I would later see on the TV documentary, *Scared Straight* based in Rahway, New Jersey. Yet history had other plans for me. I was the youngest in my family and therefore had everyone's history before me to learn from. For me, there would be no "crystal ball" to peep the future. Only direct trial and error. Hit and miss. After all, it is said: GOD WORKS IN MYSTERIOUS WAYS.

Chapter 2
Struck by Lightening

"The little girl in women die easily,
The little boy in men die hard."

(Comrade)
Assata Shakur

I recall as clear as the driven snow. One day in my life, at the tender age of five, my brothers were seeking permission to go to the park. My father gave his approval and they were off. Or almost. I flew into my father's arms and hugged him while simultaneously begging to be allowed to tag along. It was well known I would throw myself onto the floor and display tantrums that many would claim were gross exaggerations. I would crash to the floor and flop around like a fish out of water until whoever, Mom or Dad, would see it my way. My father, having enough, would instruct my brothers, Sonny Boy in the lead, to "take your lil' brother with you guys." I would run to our bedroom, snatch my coat, and we would be off.

The park, just a couple of blocks away, was called Popular Park. It was very small, but it was all we had. As we made our way, a friend joined us. As always, my big brothers made me follow my father's rules. The youngest was to be surrounded and kept in the middle at all times. We had just arrived at the corner and stopped for a moment so I could tie my shoes. All of a sudden, from nowhere, a bolt of lightning appeared. It went directly over my shoulder and hit our neighbor, Tony, in his back. At five years of age, needless to say, I was among other things totally shocked. Frightened out of my mind. I recall Tony lying there, seemingly with smoke coming from the top of his head. So, that's how we lost Tony. Struck by lightning. Had I not stopped to tie my shoe, the lightning would have hit me directly in the back of my head, so goes the story. Tony was dead before he even hit the ground. Such is how my life has been. Numerous "close calls."

We lived at 3108 Linden Street until I was six years old. My father would find a nice little home for us on the eastside of Oakland, and off we went. It was ok: a cozy little upstairs/ downstairs spot on 79th and Alder, right off of East 14th. I was like a domesticated dog taken out to the woods for the very first time: much to do and much to sniff out. A getting-to-know-you process was in full effect. Kids and families galore. Everybody had brothers and sisters. Some far more than others. My mother's sister still stayed on the west side of the "O" and Moms would often go to visit her, taking us along. We would unite with our cousins, go to the Clauson School grounds right down the street to play baseball and what not. My first encounter with the nab Jones[2] would occur at this very spot.

---

[2] Police.

As kids will do, we went to play baseball. It was summer, and school was out. Summer vacation was here. As we played, one of the guys hit a ball and it went through a classroom window. We knew they had a janitor there doing whatever he was doing somewhere on the premises. We went into the school, sought him out and endeavored to solicit his help in retrieving our hardball. To which, he nutted-up and outright refused. My cousin, Lonnie Wayne, and I became so enraged we went back down the school's stairs and outside. We came to an agreement to commence breaking all the windows within reach of the baseball bat. So, off we went in our rage, smashing windows galore. From nowhere, the janitor appeared and commenced to yell and chase after us. We broke into a sprint in every which way. For unknown reasons, the janitor set his sights on me! As I attempted to shake him, I ran around the corner of the school and tried to make it up some stairs, but he was fast on me. So much so, he tried to grab me and I jumped clear of him, tried to get around him, and back down the stairs but there was no room. I quickly shifted my feet, launched myself as best as possible, but my foot landed on his and I stumbled sideways and crashed into a window. A piece of glass the size of a 12 inch icicle went into my right side. The pain was so raw, I passed out. When regained consciousness, I was at Children's Hospital.

Come to find out, we had broken out some 18 windows—19 if you include the one I crashed through. My parents had to pay for all the damage, notwithstanding my being hospitalized, and then of course, there would be court proceedings. This was merely my first encounter with the nab Joneses. I would be "busted" exactly 21 times by my 21st birthday. Out of that 21 times, I would be arrested twice in one day. This would occur during my teens.

At this juncture of my life, every year, my parents would travel back down south to Mississippi to see family on my mother's side. She also had family in Brooklyn and Queens in New York. It was standard for us to visit. My father would drive. We loved it and looked forward to traveling and being with our cousins. Playing out in the woods, out in the fields, indulging in the sugar cane, trying to come to terms with our elders "pickin' cotton"—it was fun! Different! And, my brothers, cousins and I were always up for the challenge. Come what may.

It was that time of year again, and dear old Dad made the announcement: we were going on vacation. The grown-ups worked out a time frame for when we'd depart. We kids, as usual, continued to play and remained care-free. When things were set, the grown-ups would let us know. Until then, whatever! This particular vacation was no different from the rest, minus Pops had a new car and it was my turn to sit up front in the middle. There I could mess with the radio, inquire and insist, and just be a pest in general. The news had come from dear old Dad: soon, we'd be off to Mississippi.

Wasn't long before the day of departure was upon us. My father gave me the green light to go out to the car and warm it up. I musta' sprained both ankles getting out there. I put the key in the ignition, fired up the Bonneville, and hurried up and blast the radio. Then, I waited, listening to my favorite record at the time; "Kathy's Clown" by the Everly Brothers. Shortly thereafter, my sister, Punkin, came a-running. She knocked on the window in her normal agitated state of doing things, placed her hands on her hips, and ordered me, "Boy! Momma said get in there and help her put stuff in the car." She then set off on her mission to tell the neighbors, "We're leavin', and don't forget to watch the house 'til we get back!"

Everything was just Jim Dandy. We packed up, checked then double-checked everything. Rounded up the troops and jumped in. Finally, I'd get my sight-seeing on. I'd soon be in the company of cousins of mixed age—some the exact same age as me, others slightly older, some slightly younger. But, I simply loved the country. It was so different from where and how we lived in Oakland. There were a time or two that we got to ride horses, and once, I got to climb up on a big brown and white cow and ride it around as my cousin led it by a rope. Happy days were here again—or so I thought.

Chapter 3
Mississippi
(Play-n-Dirty Pool)

"How can I love the man who raped my mother, killed my father, enslaved my ancestors, dropped atomic bombs on Japan, killed off the Indians, and kept me cooped up in the slums? I'd rather be tied up in a sack and dropped into the Hudson River."
(Malcolm X)

I nibbled on the various food items my mother had prepared. I had a field day with the chicken, one of my favorites. My big brothers and I would often clash over the last of the chicken and Mom's scrumptious banana pudding back at home. I took in the sights of the animals grazing and just moving about. The sight of hills, mountains, animals of all sort, bodies of water, and nature in its many forms did me good. I soaked it all in as music blared from the radio. *Hit the Road Jack* by Ray Charles, one of my favorites, jammed. Then the DJ hit us with a blast by Ike and Tina Turner; *I Know It's Gonna Work Out Fine* got us squirming in our seats. It was a three day trip from the Bay Area to Mississippi. By now I had somewhat learned the way. I was about 11 or 12 on this particular trip back South, so I'd learned well the goings on between The Bay and 'Sip...

Nobody could tell me nothing. I was in heaven. I was up front, snug tight between Mom and Dad. All of a sudden, my sister went on one of her well-reputed nags for some french fries. My father, a man who could not say no to his only daughter, of course agreed to her demand and "suggestion" to pull over. We were somewhere in the state of Texas, and I'll never forget this, the longest day I've lived. It was very hot, as usual, in this part of the country at this time of year. So, when opportunity availed itself, Pops pulled into this small, makeshift, do-low looking spot. After getting us straight on exactly what he was gonna buy and not buy, he climbed out the car—ole' Bessy as he liked to call it—and set off to place the order with which to satisfy our demands, my sister in the lead. When my father returned to the car, he gave everyone their issue. Shortly after, my mother said, "This ain't nothing but onions. Ain't no meat on this." My father was terribly in love with his family, terribly in love with my mother, and anything but a coward. This, coupled with his extremely strong dislike for the whiteman, he flew into a rage. My mother, realizing what was about to happen, tried her best to persuade him to let it be, but my father was having none of it. He was well-reputed for calling the white man a "cracker." As he opened the car door, he muttered something under his breath about "them dam crackers," reached across my lap and snatched the burger from my mother. He slammed the car door and off he marched.

We watched from afar as my father exchanged words at the small fast food business. Shortly thereafter, a big whiteman emerged from the side door and approached my dear father. More words were exchanged. Then, all of a sudden, we could see more anger and agitation manifest. I commenced to scoot toward the door on my father's side so that I might jump out and join him, when my mother told me, "Boy! Don't you get out this car, you hear me?" I nodded in the affirm—active and frozen. Now, staring all the more intently. The big burley white guy was pointing at our car as if to instruct my father to return to it at once. However, that didn't happen and, knowing our father to the extent we did, knew it wasn't gonna happen, under no circumstances, period.

Then, the side door opened again. This time two more white males appeared from inside. Now it was three to one, and we were on their turf. It showed too. Both my mother in the front seat, sitting shotgun as it was called, and my sister in the back, had rolled their windows down. We could hear words such as "Nigger" and "boy" being tossed around. My father, however, stood his ground. Finally, we arrived at a point where one of the three upped and harked up, and spit in my father's face. My mother was now hysterically screaming and pleading to my father to come back to the car, when I broke for the door and totally shined my mother's decree on. I leapt out and immediately ran toward my father's side as he looked over his shoulder and started to emulate my mother's instructions for me to return back to the car. But I was determined to be by my father's side, come what may.

I froze between the car and some 15 feet or so from my father. As I stood there listening and watching, I noticed a bunch of rocks and bricks up against the side of the business. I broke toward them, snatching up a brick. I jetted toward the white dude I saw spit in my father's face and, with all the strength I could muster, threw the brick at his big, red face. I don't recall if I hit my mark or not, but I dam sho' got at him. One of the three grabbed me and this ignited my father like a powder keg. He fought with the other two, tooth and nail, while the third shoved me so violently, I went flying. Just as soon as I could gather myself I was back on my feet and launching another attack. This time, I was determined, so much so the 'wood kicked me. I took most of it on the side of my head, however some of his boot also found its way to the side of my neck. I was rendered unconscious.

When I regained consciousness, we were on the road and I was in the back seat stretched across my mother's lap. I was yelled at (told?), "Don't you e-e-ever do nothing like that, boy! And what you tryin' to do, get us all killed?" And so on and so forth. As for me, I was glad to see my dad was

A-ok. However, my neck was sore for the longest after that. Far worse than a crook in my neck was this: I could sense that, true, my parents were upset with me, but I could also tell they were proud of me for my display of courage. Lucky for us, said my father, that cracker didn't have a gun. Lucky for that cracker, I said to myself, I didn't have one. Somehow I knew that the so-called Jim Crow Law of authority was no match for political will, even at this tender age. Perhaps this was a portent of things to come. As I review my life, I have never been one to back down, come what may. On to Mississippi we rolled.

As I began to get my wits about me and stir a bit, my father said over his shoulder as he drove, " Listen, I'm gonna tell you and your sister something..."—my brothers had not come on this vacation this time as they were old enough to stay home and work summer jobs. My sister and I listened very closely to what our father had to say. It had long become clear to us that when he spoke in a certain tone, take heed, for he was not the one when it came to chastisement. By this time, we had pulled over so my mother could re-take her place in the front seat alongside my father. My sister and I huddled up between the divider of the front seat, placed our chins on our forearms and soaked in every word.

Our father told us, "A long time ago, when I got out of the Army, I came home and..." –my mother cut in and endeavored to stop him, telling him we were too young for this story. But my father would have none of it. "Aww, they 'bout ready for it—junior high," he said. "They will understand." He went on. "Your mother always been my girl. As soon as I got back to Mississippi, got stable, I asked for her whereabouts. She was working at a restaurant in Magnolia. So I gets all du' deed up and head on out there. And there she was, looking just as fine as ever. So, we talks. I knew she had eyes for me." At different intervals my mother would jump in and try to shift the flow of the conversation, if not change it altogether. But Pops was on it. On he went with telling us how he and my mother hooked up.

My father told us that he had coffee and some pancakes. They were talking it up when all of a sudden, the sheriff comes in. My father described him as a giant of a white guy. Some six feet four in height, red hair, freckles, a nasty temper and an even more nasty mouth, especially in the company of women. He came over to where my father was sitting and began to ask him about his travels in the military. My father explained that this guy, the sheriff, would not go away. He stated this guy was known from yesteryear to have eyes for my mother. He'd wink at her as well as say all kinds of sly things, and his eyes would roam. He asked my father what he intended to do now that he was out of the Army, to which my father replied that he intended to marry and settle down. "Got anybody in mind?" he asked. "Well, yeah I do," Pops replied. "Ole Martha right there. Why, we might just up and tie the knot, ain't that so Martha?" The sheriff turned red as a tomato, my father said, and his breathing became frustrated.

My father went on to tell us how the sheriff became very volatile and even more insulting. So much so, my father deemed it to be in his best interest to leave. So he said parting words to my mother and was off. The sheriff, however, had other plans. He shadowed my father outside where he told him, "Nigger, I don't ever wanna see you 'round these parts again," and issued serious threats of physical harm if his words were not carried out to the letter. My father said he didn't respond to the ol' cracker. "So the ol' cracker reached out and grabbed my shoulder, spun me around, and caught me in the head." This knocked my father to the ground, which was said to have been muddy and still sprinkin'. My father said as he attempted to get to his feet, "Why, that ol' cracka kick me in the face. So I tried to get up again, and why, he kick me again. So I was almost out. When I finally got enough strength to try to get up again, why this time, he kick me so hard I went out cold, face down. The mud got in both my nostrils, and don't be for your mother and the other sister also worked there, who turned me over on my back and cleaned out my nose, I woulda' died right there."

Pops went on to tell us, "I bide my time. It took me well over a year, but I finally got his pattern down. I watched that ol' cracker from afar for the longest. Finally, one day I got me one of them old R.C. Cola bottles and filled it halfway with water. I filled it halfway so that he would get the full impact of the blow. So, I hid behind the trunk of this big ol' tree. When that ol' sheriff came walking his everyday route, why, I waited till he walk by and I let him have it. Whoop! I cracked him in the head. He stumbled a bit but he didn't go down. So I cracked that ol' cracker again, and this time he buckled a bit but still didn't go down. So I hit that ol' cracker one mo' 'gin and this time, down he went. Skull crushed under the weight of the coke bottle."

My mother cuts in, telling my father, "That's enough," but my father was determined to tell his story. On he went. He said, "Now I'm gonna tell y'all somethin' but y'all can't go around telling nobody, y'all understand me?" My sister and I agreed. He told us that our name was not really Jackson. He told us the story as he drove on to Mississippi, how he and his brothers were thought to be the ones killed the sheriff. The incident between the sheriff and my father back at the restaurant was common knowledge. So, people made the connection between the sudden demise of the sheriff and my father as people didn't have the heart to just up and take a law man out, let alone a white one. Especially in the Deep South where everyone knew they played dirty pool. So my father and his brothers were wanted. They went underground and got the word out to the church they attended to pool money and also help get them to Louisiana, to which the people and my family complied. My father and his brothers dwelled in Louisiana for a time, then they decided to split up, change their names and regroup later. This is exactly what they did. One of my uncles went to Illinois, so I have family in that state to this day. Many I've never had a chance to meet—we know we all exist on this planet some place.

My father told us that all of his family hailed from West Africa; from the country of Ghana. They were from the Ashanti tribe, thus I took my first name in honor of my father's tribe. Let me add that I'll die with it. I could give less than a dam about a so-called slave name. Later my father taught us a culture—of sorts—among other things. Another of my uncles went to New Jersey, and to this day I have family—and mad, mad love for any brother or sister—from Jersey. My father taught us that he had what some call a "Bible name" and that his first name was really Talmus! He told my sister and me that we must never tell anyone. I relay this today because he has passed and I deem it a story worth telling. My father taught insistently that when they came from Ghana, they lived in what is today Trinidad. So, I have family on the island of Trinidad as well. Our family was forcibly made to accept the slave name "Hampton." It has been long rumored that the martyr and esteemed revolutionary Black Panther, Fred Hampton, is a direct relative of mine. We also learned from my dear father and his oldest sister, my Aunt Ruby, that we were first cousins to the world renowned revolutionary, George Jackson, who, coincidentally, was born in Chicago, Illinois. So I have revolutionary, freedom fighter, rebellious temperament and an extra healthy dose of Black Nationalism in my blood. And, I might add, I don't want no blood transfusion. I'm pleased with things just the way they are. I intend to die a freedom fighter no matter what, come what may, give a' dam about the numerical odds and/ or the risks inherently involved. I am also pleased with my father and aunt for spotlighting this information. My father also used to talk to members of the mighty Black Guerilla Family (B.G.F.) in visitation rooms at San Quentin and Tracy, aka the Gladiator School. Comrade Hashima (x-Michael Murdock) was called Doc until 1977 when we received political decrees to change our slave names. Hashima would ask my father pressing questions about George, my uncle Robert Lester, and their father (my grandfather), Jonathan.

In reality, there was a logical reason why George didn't care for whites. And, should you come to an understanding of my family history, you will likely concur. There has historically been naught but bad experiences between the forked-tongue fold and my family as well as my tribe overall. George knew this all too well. Not only did he know of it, he actually "understood" what he knew. Understanding is paramount. It is only natural for me to harbor mad love for the city of Chi-town and, of course, Patterson, New Jersey, across to the George Washington Bridge into New York, particularly Brooklyn and Queens—all locations where I have family. My father bequeathed all this information and more as we rolled toward Mississippi. When we arrived, we learned more still. For example, my father's father—whose real name was Edgar!—was a very strong advocate of the Garvey philosophy. Before coming to Mississippi, he attended meetings headed up by Noble Drew Ali speaking on the Moorish Science Temple of America. My grandfather Edgar would become annexed to Medgar Evers, their friendship lasting both their lifetimes. One example of their close tie involved the harassment of a sister in Jackson, Mississippi by two service station attendants. When news of the happenings reached Evers and my grandfather, they climbed into my grandfather's truck and went to the station to pay the two harassers a visit. They pulled into the Union 76 gas station, sought out the culprits and duly cautioned the both of them. The warnings ensued with the words, "IF SHE IS EVER BOTHERED AGAIN, YOU WILL PAY AND THE PRICETAG WILL BE BLOOD." Exactly 14 days later, both Brother Evers and my grandfather were killed. Evers would be killed on my birthday while my grandfather, Edgar, disappeared without a trace—his truck, the shotgun they brandished at the two attendants, all gone and vanished to this day. It was always said that George took this very hard and was forever bitter because of it. One of my brothers, who used to sing back-up for R&B singer Sam Cooke, sang a song about these events that never received airplay—just like the deeds of the x-Jacksons being down and fighting for human rights, dignity, and the like. All swept under the rug. My grandfather, so we were led to believe, was said to have been thrown into the swamps. All we know for certain is that my beloved grandfather disappeared without a trace along with the aforementioned truck and shotgun. I might also add, like my cousin George Lester Jackson, whom some of us prefer to call "Amin Ali," I too am hella pissed off at those responsible for the demise of any of mine. Now, and forever.

    We arrived in Mississippi without further incident, unloaded the car and settled in. When my father reported what transpired in the state of Texas, no one was really surprised. They were more so concerned about me and my neck, which was purplish-blue and badly swollen. Nonetheless, I survived. Like that ol' bunny, still going. My family survived being uprooted from West Africa and taken to Trinidad, then onto "the States," so survival was in my genes. I am descendant from the Ali's. Nab Jones and cohorts have endeavored to break the chain, but we have managed to keep our history covert and bequeath it accordingly. I and an x-socialized HAMPTON come JACKSON, yet knowingly, in reality, I am an Ali. Ashanti Ali!

Chapter 4
Back on the Block
(Pimps and Punks)

"The few think kindly of the thinking few,
The many don't think but think they do."
(Commander: Ho Chi Minh)

Once we returned to Oakland things seemed to accelerate. Before you know it, you're in junior high and have your very first locker. Hall and gym lockers tend to usher in trouble of sort, especially where I'm from. I have always been one to seldom forget and hold a grudge for a lifetime. Such be the case for the white boy who kicked me in my neck yesteryear. Sooner or later, somebody, someday was gonna pay, in part due to all the information on my family that I now carried wherever I went.

During our sojourn in Mississippi we would sit around the giant wooden table and share stories. When it came time for my mother to speak, I recall her telling how her twin sister, Mary, was snatched by four whites and taken deep into the woods. She would be found some 27 days later. The wild animals and insects had done such a job on her she was not truly recognizable. That stung. Till this day, I harbor ill-will unto those responsible and those still partisan to such deeds. But, before I arrived at my contemporary position and outlook, I was of a totally different ilk.

Back on the block in Oakland I had become a fully functioning member of a gang; the Am-Boy-Dukes. The Dukes for short. Am-Boy because the gang, as it were, was founded by my big homie Am Kelly. So the gang was his. We wore red. Many don't know about the Dukes of Oakland, especially those down south (L.A.) but the Dukes were in effect back in '58, '59 and well in the '60s. The difference was Bloods from Oakland (the Dukes) were all about hand (duke-n-it-out). There was no such thing as using guns. No treason/ very little inner-circle conflict. And certainly we were never so foolish as to allow a whiteboy into our gang. Save it! We were extremely tight, wore our red bandanas proudly and, quiet as kept, this had a direct bearing on why brothers from Oakland—not the Bay Area, but OAKLAND—had a natural affinity towards Bloods from down south. Brothers from Oakland and Bloods from L.A. tend to gravitate towards one another. They formed an alliance to wage combat with whosoever endeavored to sever that bond. Only here of late these youngsters of today, from wherever—Inglewood, Hub City (Compton-Ru's), Bounty Boys, etc.—we always got along until a new generation sprung up with absolutely no schooling or reputable leadership. Things fell apart. Some Bounty Hunters I must give credit to have made attempts—with some success—to rekindle the fire that once burned between damus and kept us all warm. This, I know because I've been in dialogue with them myself. The problem is with the youngsters, yet I know they can be reached.

So, early on, I flagged red. Red as red can get, and then some. We were "Ave. Boys." Jesse Davis was brutal. His brother, Ricky, would fight anything that bleed or breathe. Stan Williams (Popeye), a true hog, not to mention Roman Williams, Simon Vonn, and Kevin Williams. Well known for throwing down. I mentioned Am Kelley, but his younger brothers my age, give or take a year of two, was perhaps the most vicious, and certainly the most feared. Then Henry and Roy, and their two brothers my age, Lindell (Knockem Down) and Greg (Rubber Duck), had major hands. Irving Washington, my boy was sick. We often called Irv "Speed" because he was so quick. Michael "Foots" Johnson, a hog for real, James "J-Rod" Smith, had power galore and a no nonsense temper to match. James and Tony Stanley, heart be the word. Lynch couldn't really squab but down for whatever and a pure-dee hustler. Keith and Kenny Gallon, every now and then. Cool, calc, but will do you in a heartbeat, especially Keith. There were too many Dukes to count. We had our hats and would often let our red rags hang from them and bail throughout the hood.

It was not long before I had become a full-fledged burglar, car thief, purse snatcher—and this was only for starters. I rose fast to the top of the Dukes primarily because of my hands and my heart. It has been said, "IF HE KNEW BETTER, HE'D DO BETTER!" How true. As a kid, you go with the flow. Whatever manifest, you engage it. As a youth, you never think about consequences, at least not until you get caught.

Minus a crystal ball to see what was coming, I rolled with my boys. One time, we were hanging in the back of Castlemont, or the Castle as we called it. It is the major high school of the east side of Oakland. There exist numerous other high schools: Freemont, Skyline, Oakland High and a host of adult day high schools located on the east side. The north side only had one; Tech. On the west side, they only had one; Mack. That's it and that's all. We clashed every time we bumped. Mostly over stupid stuff such as who won the football or basketball game. Often we would actually go so far as to turn their bus over, hindering their transportation back to their side of the town. We engaged in a game called "Dare!" to the extent we became out of control. It may start with a simple dare to break every single car antenna visible with no exception, despite anyone witnessing such or whatever, outside watering their lawn. It didn't matter. If we decided upon a street, any car visible became a target. This included if being chased. If such was the case, you had to run in such wise where you to go in circles and yet break all car antenna visible. Eventually we evolved, so to speak. We would later commence to target any and all whitefolk's homes with a picture window. This became one of my favorites. Never once did we stop to entertain thought of just how hard those people had worked to purchase such a house. We simply didn't have anything else or better to do. So, picture windows we agreed upon, and picture windows it was. And man did we straight smash many. All the way from First Avenue and 98th. If they had the gall to put up cardboard, we'd bide our time, catch them slipping (sleeping or gone) and douse the cardboard or lighter fluid, whatever was available, and blaze be the word. We wanted them to move, which was our objective; we wanted nothing but Blacks in the neighborhood. If they fixed the picture window, we'd hang tight, catching them laggin' and do it alllll over again. This was done 'til they moved.

When we moved from 79th to 73rd, I made new potnas. I still got out and about with the Dukes, but it was getting old. People, like Brother Mark Comfort, who happened to stay right behind us, or on the other side of the fence, would often call all the young brothers into his garage and tell us about his future plans. He had printing equipment, was exceptionally articulate, and had his own pad—complete with a white girl no less—and a son our age, Danny, who had a temper himself. Mark used to tell us all sorts of stuff about history, and in particular, the history of the South. Mark, who by now, had met and fully embraced my father, would send us out to "round up" the young brothers to come and listen. We'd meet up in Mark's garage (until my father built an extra room onto his garage) and would learn about lynchings, death by fire, death by drowning, death by impalement...I was learning that in fact, my father knew a lot about a lot he had not exposed my family to. Now we were all ears, and more importantly, we were fast becoming serious. At least some of us far more than others.

At this time, we hadn't moved to the north side yet, but one day we would—right next door to my potna Huey P. Newton. But for now, I was still on the east side doing dirt, as it were. In and out of jail be the word. Once, while up at the Castle shooting dice, the police came. They were always employing new tactics which meant we were learning about tactics. This time, they had us cut off at both ends and also had pigs in the creek just in case we hit the fence—we were known to get away thus. I would be caught, taken to juvenile hall and my mother'nem would come and get me out about three that evening. I listen to them preach to me about this and that and so on and so forth. It didn't even penetrate one ear, let alone out the other. My mind was on getting back to my boys, flexing, being I'd been to jew-v yet again, and doing even more dirt. That night, I commenced to get ready to go a party thrown by my home girl, Yvonne. Moms protested vehemently, but I assured them I had learned my lesson and would be trouble free. Plus, she was one of the most popular sisters at school, fine as May wine, and had got me directly, face-to-face, to come and dance with her. I was known to get down on the dance floor, no jive. So, after much ado, Moms gave in and let me go. Off I went.

I met up with my cousin, Rusty, and my then best friend, Kenny Frazier. We slid to the party and had a ball. We somehow got our hands on a few rolls of reds (reds or red devils, as there were also called, are a depressant, or "downer"). Very potent. We each took hella reds while drinking Old English, some Rainer Ale, and a drop of 151. Plus a gang of weed. In short, the norm. After the party, which was in the 80s block, we had a good walk back to our hood. Our collective attitude back then: fuck that! I had all sorts of "master keys" I had swiped from my probation officer who had the nerve to leave me alone in his office like I wasn't gonna see what come-up was available. Some b52s (master keys) to steal cars with. Need I say more? A car was in need so a car it was indeed.

We bickered about who should drive. Everybody claimed to be too loaded to drive, and we were outside somebody's residence, so we had to move the crowd now. I said, "Fuckit, I'll drive." I staggered round to the driver's side, hit the door with my b52s and was in. Unlock the door for Ken and Russ and we were off. Same thing we be after a James Brown concert at the Oakland Auditorium. I was loaded, truth be told. I don't remember much, only when I regained consciousness, the police were everywhere, including one with his foot on my throat.

Later, I would be made aware that I had run a red light, hit a car, which caused me to run into the red-light pole. That caused me to crash into an Arco gas station at about 60 to 80 miles an hour and straight took out a gas pump. Knocked the gas pump totally off its foundation. It evidently was the Creator of the createds' plan for it not to go up in flames. It won't mention the money my parents had to pay for the car, county property (the red-light pole), and of course, the gas station mess to say the least. Think I had finally learned my lesson? Being busted twice in one day was no big thang, just added to my so-called "rep." Fact is, I hadn't even got started.

As I advanced into my teens, I showed out so much that I never again received the opportunity to return to Mississippi. Mississippi was replaced with trips to juvenile halls. And, as it would not be too long before the trips to "jew-v" would be replaced with frequent trips to both city and county jails.

Unlike most of the brothers my age I was known to associate with, I took the lessons and information passed down to us in those garages of past times very serious. This information, coupled with both direct and indirect experiences, caused me to become unglued.

While discretion may well be the better part of valor, to me I was learning that, oftentimes, deception was not. I would often cut school and hang out with my big homies, Rod and Jeff Smith, when they were not in prison. Likewise with my G-homie, Eldridge Cleaver, who was always up for imparting information to us to us youngsters as well as just engaging in conversation. And boy did Eldridge have stories to tell. He often bragged about his contributions to the people's struggle, and how he paid the "Ofays" (a term radicals used in the 60s for white people) back for what they did to us during slavery. It was absolutely fascinating. Many Panthers disapproved of Eldridge, however, there were certainly some that approved.

Eldridge, as he entailed in his best seller, "Soul On Ice," took pure delight in telling us how he would "coldtrail" jezebels (white women) from places such as super markets, downtown, even churches and so forth and monitor their habits. He then would kidnap them in some cases, in others he'd play into their life and, I quote him verbatim, would fuck them in the ass, then make them lick their very own shit off of his dick and then swallow it. He'd fall back into laughter. He told those stories to many—sometimes up at Groove Street College where radicals hung out, and sometimes up at the Lamp Post, a club reported be owned by the Black Panthers. I know for certain they were always present and they maintained control of their turf. They tolerated absolutely no nonsense on the property. The Lamp Post was on the north side on a corner. I was too young, according to law, to go inside, yet I often snuck in anyway.

It was, in fact, Eldridge, who told us about Steve Biko. Up to that point, I had never heard of Biko. We were told how the white racist there in South Africa broke every single bone in Biko's body. Every bone. This was carried out systematically, to inflict as much pain as possible. Often Eldridge, Huey, or any other number of brothers that particular day, would bequeath information about situations and incidents and outright murders of people such as Brother Emmitt Till, of Chicago. And, being Emmitt was a Chicago native, I was naturally fond of him and deeply upset when I learned of his fate. We would hear of the Civil Rights activists that were also killed in Mississippi on my birthday—two whites and one Black—later found buried, etc. We would learn of the fate of the Scottsboro Boys, so-called, and how the white girl lied on them, swearing they gang raped her, only to recant her words long after they all had been imprisoned. No apology to the families given whatever. Some of what was being imparted I was able to digest and process, some was too raw. This "raw" portion caused others and myself to commence to strike out at people of European descent. I thought to myself from time to time, the sheer nerve of them publishing material about this lil' peck-ass-punk, Willie Lynch. I used to tell a great number of people I wish I could've run into this buster Willie Lynch. Yeaaaaa buddy!

Thus we would set off, unbeknownst to our parents, to right these wrongs inflicted on our kith and kin. We often would break every car window on some white folks in "our" neighborhood. Or, we would make a direct assault. One guy lived by himself, directly in the middle of our hood. The nerve of him, we felt. So time and again, we would wait on ole' John to leave for work, or someplace else, and we would break into his house, smash everything smashable, break everything breakable, plug the toilet with whatever, stop up the bathtub and turn the water on full blast. Same for the kitchen sink; flood the place. Smeared condiments of sorts on the walls. Later, after some three attempts to "run him out" failed, we then employed arson. Finally, John got the message and vanished into thin air.

These type of exploits, however, were not good enough for some of us. Me heading the list of those yet discontent and wanting even more direct action. After all, it was mother's twin sister who was raped, sodomized, poison forced down her throat, then her panties forced down her esophagus. I had learned of some of my kinfolk outright murdered by whitefolk in Mississippi long before I was even born. Injustices were innumerable. And, it would be just such a situation involving one of my big brothers. This time, it was Sonny Boy. Our oldest and the most vicious with his hands. He and Comrade George could pass for twins. Sonny was buying something at the local store when, we were told, he allegedly leaned on the glass counter and it caved in, resulting in a large piece of glass lodged in my brother's eye. After the dust settled, the store owner didn't wanna help in any way or have anything more to do with the incident. My parents had gone there and talked to them repeatedly with regards to my brother possibly going to lose his sight in one eye. No avail. On and on until, finally, pops just let it go. I thought not...

I took it upon myself to watch the store close for a time. After I felt I knew their pattern, the waiting kicked in. Finally, opportunity availed itself. I had a 2' x 4' with nails in it. When the peck came out and was locking the metal outside the part of his business, I crept up on him and bashed him in the head with the 2' x 4'. Got his ass, I thought. I split and went my way.

Chapter 5
LOOK + LISTEN = LEARN

"The mind is like a parachute: it works best when it's open."
(Comrade George)

Like a shark that's tasted blood, I had not only exacted some measure of payback but also, and perhaps most importantly, I liked the feeling it gave. Now, it was on in the worst way.

I learned from Eldridge Cleaver the word *norkim*, which meant avenger in Hebrew. I never forgot it or its meaning. He also schooled me with regard to "Jews" and how they were more serious about their kith than anybody on Earth. So much so, Jews were known to hunt down Nazis as old as 80, and a few slightly older still, to snatch them covertly and take them back to have their day in court. Often they brought or returned these Nazis back to Germany to be tried for war crimes and crimes against humanity. It is well documented how Jews sought those deemed responsible for the 1943 extermination which occurred in Warsaw, Poland. For this I applaud the Jews. Make no mistake.

Jews track Nazis down around the world, never once becoming weary. Such is the love for their people the Jew displayed for the whole world to see. Repeatedly, mind you. Certainly a matter of record. I was deeply impressed. Only thing was, I had not the wherewithal to engage in such activity. I had to work with what I had: the will to manufacture targets, whoever, as long as they were ofay. I totally refused to "stop" at begging for reparations like most of my tribe. Being that I couldn't track down those who had killed off much of my tribe who were still vertical, and there being no recourse minus what today would amount to random liquidations, I decided to make AmeriKKKan ofays pay.

Eventually, time would cast me in the minds of many. I had become known for tossing an old man out of his wheelchair, and for kicking the crutches out from under an old man in broad day light. Fun to me it was not; this was sheer, raw, justifiable payback! It could be summed up in a quote from Brother Eldridge: WAR! The Nazis that had run to Argentina and Brazil and so forth who felt they were out of reach, untouchable as it were, felt they had pulled off the great horrible holocaust minus consequence. No! No! No! Hell naw! In my short time on Earth, I had seen too much. Heard even more. Knew that no one was really doing anything whatsoever about our war here in the hells of North AmeriKKKa. Then came me! Nobody ever born—and I mean nobody—ever hated the white race like me. So much so, I am going to purposely state that again. NOBODY EVER WALKED THE EARTH HATED THE WHITE RACE

LIKE ME. They were yet to be born. I would in time become the Black Josef Mengele.

I recall clear as the driven snow the very first person I shot. He was an insurance man. They used to come to your home back in the 50s and 60s. They were known for having much cash on their person as a result of folks paying them up front. This person, mid-30ish, was putting money in a parking meter. I told my homies, "Watch this!" I trotter towards him, blasted him one time dead in the face, did an about face, and sprinted back to the stolen Nova. We laughed it up and smoked more weed. I had struck gold, so to speak. I had broken into his home and found numerous weapons, including a .22 (it shot .22 shells). I carried it everywhere I went from that point on, and it was a known fact. I commenced to black[3] whitefolks almost at random. I was my own boss and I answered to no one, regardless.

At this juncture in history, Oakland was scalding hot. Watts's riot had set shit off some of everywhere. Oakland was no exception. It was totally commonplace to turn a corner and walk head-on into "pigs" and a brother or brothers, fighting like Jews and Muslims in a phone booth. Often, the first chance we get we'd rush in and open the back door of the pig's car and set whoever free. If we could, we knew how to keep the pigs occupied while whoever made their getaway. Handcuffed or not because we had the means all throughout every hood to get brothermen out of some cuffs, if not but cut the shit off his wrists.

We made it standard to go up on ramps and give the signal, and so-and-so would call and have CHP (California Highway Patrol) come to that particular freeway, normally the Nimitz because of where it is located. We knew the ramps and hoods like the back of our hands, and we knew each and every parent—the strict and the liberal—and when they be at home and when they were at work. We'd blast at CHP cars and cut out. Sometimes, when a bit younger, we'd do the same to bus drivers too. The second person I ever shot was a taxi driver. I shot him in the back of the head returning from a concert. This, for absolutely no other reason than he was white and got caught at the wrong time and place...by me. My name rang like a church house bell on Sunday morning, especially on the eastside. I used to beg and plead with Huey to "let me be one of the sisters' bodyguard." The answer was always no! So I did my own thing. Even went

---

[3] Scream, yell, to go off. *http://urbandicitonary.com*

to the extent to form a tightknit group, or gang if you will, and set out to terrorize folk all the more. I didn't care!

I kept it real simple: if we ran across whoever and the opportunity avail itself, jump out, blast his ass, and cut out. Sometime, 'pending where we are, we would run them over, put the car in reverse, run them over backwards, put the car in drive, gun it, run them over yet again, and keep going, never even looking in the rearview mirror. I had not a clue but, surely as sunset, I was getting way out of control. And, what was so cold, out of fear my boys wouldn't dare say anything in terms of checking me. I raged on.

One day, a Sunday evening to be specific, I was sitting on the front porch with my boy, Vic, just kicking it. We talked about what all we had did, should have did, could've did, and shouldn't have did. When along came "Bra!", slave name Lorenzo Long. But everybody just called him plain ole "Bra!" He was about four years older than us. A cold, reputed hustler. Also somewhat of an alcoholic. But he was tight with my brother, CJ, and in addition to that, above and beyond, he had jokes. He'd talk about anybody like a dog and everybody knew it. Bra kept weed and often something to sip on. He was the big homie, and seem to have had a habit of popping up out of nowhere.

He slid up, dap with us, and started in on us: "Fuck you lookin' at? Titty-headed nigga," and "Seen ya momma going to church, carrying a Bible with no hands," and on and on he'd go. We'd laugh hysterically. And the more we laughed, the more he'd talk. Then, he started in on how he just "hit-a-lick."[4] He pulled out some weed and fired up a joint. All the big homies had learned it was wise to smoke and drink with us because they knew the amount of dirt we did and that we had dope and cash more often than not. So Bra blazed with us. It would be during the course of smoking weed that his silver lighter ran out of fluid. We got up and headed off towards the store in our hood right around the corner on 73rd and Weld. Bra purchased a can of Ronson's Lighter Fluid in the blue and yellow can. He also got some red Ripple. We walked to Arroyo Park and went to the puppet house, as we called it, sat around and got loaded off the gill.

After some time we parted company. However, before doing so, we

---

[4]To do a job (usually illegally) to get money. *https://www.urbandictionary.com*

begged Bra to leave us a joint. After a lil' friendly persuasion, he agreed. And being that we didn't have any fire on us, I told him to let us use the lighter and that I'd bring it by his crib later on, which he did. Then, to my surprise, while we talked shit as he walked away, he turned around, came back and threw the can of lighter fluid, saying, "Y'all can keep it. Umma get some matches at the store on my way back 'cause I gotta get some more Zags!" [5]

We were set now. A lil' drink still left and a fat-ass joint! Vic and I chopped at it some more and finally decided to go on home as it was getting kind of late. I tucked the can of lighter fluid in my back pocket and we set off for the pad. Vic and I stayed only eight houses from one another. Vic had become my absolute best friend. When we moved to seven-tre—as we called our hood 73rd—he and I were seldom seen apart. We did everything together. If one of us didn't' have a date any particular night, then we both didn't. We sexed broads down together, robbed, stole, lied and cheated, went to every music concert that we wanted to that came to the Bay Area, especially Frisco's "Wonderland!" We did it all. Nobody could take Victor's place. I'd straight kill for that dude. Never, in my wildest dreams did I ever imagine that, in the not too distant future, my best friend Victor Darnell Jackson, would tell the police that I (allegedly) killed three people. And testify to the same. Yet one never knows what the future holds. A page of history about to be read.

I also never dreamt that, someday, we'd both have kids. In addition, no one could have ever told me that Vic would one day kill his very own son. High off "angel dust," he'd beat his infant son to death with a cane.

At his point, the Am-Boy Dukes, for all intents and purposes, had become defunct. We found ourselves in a sort of mental tug-of-war with the Black Muslims right there in our hood, with their giant temple right next door to Castlemont High. Only the "creek" separated the temple from the castle. Each time we'd go up to the castle, normally to either cop weed, shoot dice, or jam up some females, we'd have to encounter Black Muslims on the scene, selling papers, and giving vicious spills[6] about the "Yacubian" theory and that the white man is the devil.

---

[5] Zig-Zag rolling papers used to roll cigarettes.

[6] To vent, use a lot of words, free form rap. Can be positive or negative. *Source* http://urbandictionary.com

If we went up to the castle, coming from the Aves, wed' have to travel through Panther turf. "Heard about what them pecks did to them sisters in Alabama, young brothers? If not, why don't y'all pull over and let us run it down to you?" Sometimes we'd peep what they spill about, sometimes not. 'Pended upon what was on our own agenda. But, we had Panthers and Muslims at us anytime we left the house. "Listen here, little brother, I know your brothers, cousins or somebody you know, who got beat down by them pigs. Maybe your father? Maybe even you?" Sometimes I'd be too lit[7] to fully comprehend what was being said to me or asked of me to reply to. So, I'd just nod and keep it moving. Yet, I learned as the years came and went. Once an incident occurred in which the pigs shot and killed Skip older brother of some of my homies, Lindell and Greg. They shot him off a roof. People everywhere didn't look the way it went down and, as far as the neighborhood was concerned, it was cold-blooded murder, because the pigs knew he was unarmed; just being rebellious. Lethal force was totally out of the question. The "pigs" had offed big Skip.

When I emerged from my dear mother's womb, the house we stayed in was on the west side of Oakland: 3108 Linden Street. Thus I was born on the west side of the "O"…and knew many people there as well as maintained ties. Had family there as well. My mother's sister and her family, to say the least. But I grew up on the east side of Oakland. That was my stomping grounds. And, despite my love for the homies Lindell and Greg losing their brother Skip the way they did, that didn't strike a chord in me as when, right after Skip's murder, pigs took out my very close friend, Bobby Hutton. We simply called him "Lil Bobby." This took place on the west side. We were on the east. But, Lil Bobby, he was with us wherever we went, then, now and future. Perhaps that was the last straw. We also heard that the pigs had caused a fire next door to the home they assaulted my comrades at. I didn't really know brother-Comrade David Hilliard, only seen him around, never really engaged in dialogue with him like I did Huey and Big El (Eldridge). Yet the love was there. More important, I was fed up. If the pigs thought they were gonna get away with offin' my potnah Lil Bobby, shiiiiittt! It was time for a new get-down. I decided to take it to'um like never before.

---

[7] Very intoxicated. *Source http://urbandictionary.com*

I summoned my crew. Laid out a plan. We decided to start on the west side being that's where the enemy camp did Lil Bobby at. So, the west side it was. We caught a woodchuck[8] coming out the hood liquor store. Major violation. No wood was e-v-e-r to be anywhere near our hood—east side or west—when it was dark. Especially all alone. I played up on him while Vic and Ronnie Brown watched from the car. I ask ol' boy, "Do ya got a light?" He said, "No, sorry I can't help!" I pulled my .22, put it in his face and told him, "Oh! You can help alright! Walk, motherfucka!" Put him in the back seat and off we went to the east side. We took turns burning him with our cigarettes.

When we reached our chose destination, I ordered him out. We always bound and gagged anybody with our red bandanas and forced a tennis ball in their mouth. This became routine. We ordered him out, directed him accordingly, and when we were satisfied with our location, we wasted no time. For some reason, I had brought along the lighter fluid I had been given by big homie, Bra. I beat him unconscious. Squirted the lighter fluid in his face, aiming inside his nostrils and then his ears. Then, to be 100% sure, I put the tip into his ear and squeezed. Raised up, lit a match, dropped it on his face. It made a "VOOF" type of sound. He shook in convulsions as we lit cigarettes, laughed and watched—until the smell became more than we could bear.

I do not know if this man ever made it. At that point in my life, I didn't look at the news nor stop long enough to read the newspapers. Our only concern: payback! From that point on, I made it a point to keep a can of gas in my trunk, and sometimes lighter fluid in my glove compartment. Next, we would come across a female in Berkeley, our favorite hunting grounds. This because people were so overly friendly. Females, hitch-hikers, would readily approach your vehicle stopped at a red light, stop sign or otherwise, and ask for a ride. So, they became our favorite targets. Hitch-hikers. White, female hitch-hikers! On one such occasion, probably the first, we spot one such "Jezebel" in hippy-like attire. We bust a U-turn, swing around and pick her up. Once in the car, there was no escape. This time it was Vic, Ronnie and me. I would sometimes drop them off around the corner from the prospect victim-to-be, and once she was in the car, I'd drive straight to the corner and whoever was with me on that particular

---

[8] Redneck, hick, hillbilly. *Source http://urbandictionary.com*

mission, they knew to rush the door, forcing her directly in the middle, surrounded by males with guns...and attitudes. Serious attitudes. Death in our eyes. Anything but a joke.

We did not engage in rape. We all had girlfriends galore. We wasn't interested in "going 'up' in a 'bel," no! We wanted to make them suffer as the pigs had did Lil Bob and countless others. We took this particular female, like usual, to the east side. In the deep east. Blindfolded and gagged, she was ushered out of the car, taken to a secluded spot, rendered totally unconscious (knocked the fuck out as we called it), then I'd have both Vic and Ronnie take her clothes off from the waist down. "Strip her ass, nigga," I'd say. The homies would fall right in without delay. Stripped and unconscious, I'd order them to position her where absolutely no part of her body would be touching the earth except her shoulder blades. "Gap that bitch's legs, nigga. Open'num wide nigga," I'd say. "I don't want no pussy hair nigga. I know da'diffrence tween pussy hair and a pussy nigga. I don't want no dam pussy lips either, nigga. I know the difference tween pussy lips and a pussy, black ass nigga. Get'um open, nigga. Hur'up!" I'd bark out. Totally serious. This, they totally knew. Thus they fully cooperated.

On this occasion, I had gasoline. I made more than sure the gas entered (and drenched) her vagina. Then, as always, I made double sure. Poured gas on a shammy rag I brought for the occasion, took major concern to see to it that it was in fact completely doused, so much so, it was dripping gas. Then I took a stick I brought along for the occasion, and forced the shammy rag up her vagina. All but enough to set on fire. Completed, I gave the order: "Blaze that bitch!" And with that, Vic lit a match, dropped it meticulously on the rag. It too made a "VOOF" type sound. She shook violently. We watched for a bit, again until the smell was too much. We turned and walked back to my ride. Have absolutely no idea what became of her. Nor did we care. She and the event was "water under the bridge." I concerned myself with slavery; that so-called lynching bullshit, folks that had the same skin color as those who jumped my beloved father, spit in his face, knocked him out and left him in the mud, nostrils full of mud, to die or whatever! Folks that raped my mother's twin sister. Did unspeakable things to her. Four woodchucks. Never caught, despite their identity being known throughout Magnolia. Being brought to justice was unheard of. You were simply just "another dead nigga!" There was not such a thing as justice and fair play. We knew firsthand, if you wanted justice, go get it ya'dam-ness....or pee like ah bitch! Us, me and mine, we decided to go get it our'dam-ness!

With the event of "females being found with they cockhole set on fire" being the talk of the town, the Panthers, not the Muslims, really became upset, claiming we were bringing too much heat. Shiiittt, we had only blazed seven devils. Six females and one male. The male was the first victim. After that, we hit all females. Being that we were from 73rd, we initially agreed to blaze 73 females.

I spotlight this horrid behavior because, as I told those in the group I attended here at this prison, when my turn came to stand and introduce myself, I told those present: "My name is Ashanti Ali. I am a revolutionary. My addiction, some say, is the worst type of addiction to have. I AM ADDICTED TO TELLING THE TRUTH." The entire audience fell super quiet....and listened.

Our next victim would set off concern in all northern California. We made it a point to show no mercy. We had also learned from watching "Untouchables" starring Robert Stack to never hesitate when you have the drop. Do it and be done with it. Why talk? All of my homies knew way, way, way up front if they so much as dared to "kickit" with the victim, I'd blast a hole in them with no hesitation. We clocked and jocked her. And shonuff, she bit for the line I spit. "Move, bitch. Don't look at me. Just move ya' fuckin' feet." To which the "nun" fully complied. To the east side we went. Same'o. Only this time, I also stuffed a totally doused shammy rag of gas up her asshole as well as her vagina. Soaked both. Totally. Dropped a match, watched for a hot second and we split. Her, we heard about. She was found the next day.

To let it cool off, we decided to go to the Muslim meetings for a bit. There, we listened to the minister speak about all sorts of topics. The most interesting was when he went into the good ole Christian Bible and spoke in depth about homosexuality. Of this, there was no room for refute. It was a clear cut case. Both Vic and I readily agreed, males should engage females and females only. We further agreed and shook on it that to do otherwise (for a male to interact with another male) is to, among other things, cheat the female out her innate rights. We decided to not address females tripping with other females, but concerned ourselves only and specifically with the fags. Of this we were taught from childhood: keep it simple. Always keep it simple. They be PUNKS!!

We listened to the minister speak about so-called male opportunists. Of which he would employ the term PIMPS! We were told, and fully agreed until this very moment, there is nothing lower than a so-called pimp except a punk. Pimps and punks had to go. We redirected our focus and launched a new war. A war to rid Oakland, if indeed not the entire Bay Area, of pimps and punks.

Being that we now would be addressing and "hitting" new targets and trippin' a new issue, we also decided that we would employ our proper castigation methods i.e. use weapons befitting. So, regarding the so-called would-be pimp, he used his mouth to convince and sway females, so my signature was to shoot them in the mouth. We would watch for them. They (the so-called pimps) oftentimes would pull up in the park on San Pablo, on the west side near the California Hotel, well reputed and referred to as the "Ho-Stroll!" So, there we would dwell for a spell. Run a lil' some-some up the ole flag pole and see if anybody salute. And, salute they did.

I caught so many so-called pimps off guard, lagging or slipping, as it was known, it was pathetic. After shooting three so-called pimps in their mouth, right there on the west side, it became very hot. Police was still rolling deep trying to find who was setting them Jezebels on fire. Now all of a sudden, pimps were being found, being rushed to the nearest hospital, with gunshot wounds to the mouth.

Oakland had become way too hot. We decided to switch up and branch out. Frisco here we come. San Francisco was far easier and with a much bigger "stroll." So, we commence to wear it out. We used to slide up on them, parked on the strip in north beach, and holler, "Ay man. Dig, I got 20. You know me, don't you man? I'm from SD (Sunnydale)," or we'd say Mountain View, whatever came to mind. Flash dude the twoomp bill, and he'd say, "You nigga ass nigga. You! You 'da bitch." Then I'd point my gun directly at his face. It would dawn on him exactly who I was and what time it was. "Open ya mouth nigga." If he refused, or said absolutely anything, anything whatsoever, I'd just blast him in the mouth straight through the lips and/ or teeth, and be out. Fuck'em.

We soon wore Frisco out. Started hittin' the 'ho-stroll in Alameda. Wore them out in no time flat, plus they have very few prostitutional streets. They mostly dealt in escorts. Next, we moved on to San Leandro. Bet'not catch a so-called pimp out and about. Not his ass, no, hell naw. His mouth was MINE. Then we hit up Hayward. Tore a hole in it. Hayward was a mixture of pimps. A lot of Hispanics. They think they the shit. However, when you get the drop on someone, they tend to hurry up and get some act-right. Soon we was hitting up every known 'ho-stroll in the entire Bay Area. It was so hot, we started travelling as far as Stockton, and later still, Sacramento. Sacramento had the biggest stroll after San Francisco. We still maintained our goal of blasting 73 pimps. We were well on our way. However it was hot. Scalding. So, we took a self-imposed recess, went back to my father's garage, got caught up on the latest goings-ons, discussed what we had done, what we had caused, what we should do next. We concluded without a lengthy discussion, it was time to direct our displeasure with what some call PUNKS! Regarding them, we decided to simply kill.

It was agreed and firmly kept intact that, there is absolutely nothing on this planet worse than a PUNK! We hated punks with no end in sight. They were to receive absolutely no mercy. Any form of sympathy displayed or so much as detected by me and I would turn on those deemed guilty of this colossal infraction. Shooting them on the spot. I always shot homies in the thigh—the thigh because I knew they would survive, and simultaneously, they would get the message. We sometimes would blast on the Jim Jones followers, too. They were a bit rowdy and known to fight back and/ or give chase. We shot quite a bit of them. Some eight or nine, if memory serves correctly.

It was too hot. The entire Bay Area was way too hot. From learning and watching others, we knew how to chill. Go engage something else and, later, when things cool down, start the shit back up again. War had been declared on punks (fags) and so, war it would be.

Sometime later, we had learned to park. Park over and get on foot. Punks, especially Frisco punks, would tend to be not so alert, and greed (need for money) would cause them to gamble and approach you, endeavoring to solicit you for money. Yeah right! I had something for they ass alright. For the punks, we had agreed to snatch them up, slide back to the town (Oakland) and dust they ass—point blank. The key hard part, if you will, was to slick that ass into your car. Or, create a situation where they see if they can bip or bop, they was through.

A good time, we discovered, was right after a concert. Punks galore would be out and about in North Beach. Prancing hither and yon, in all their glory. And me and mine waiting on that ass. Gun always fully loaded. For punks, however, we would not shoot them in the mouth like the so-called pimp. No! Instead we would sometimes situate them to the point we would shoot them directly in their asshole. Pointblank. This, of course, if we didn't kill them outright. Sometimes, 'pending on the situation, we would set them on fire, conducted in such wise where, if they survived, we knew that (a) they would not be able to have sex again, and even if they did, they would be so ugly from the burns, it would be hard for them to become desirable; (b) even after a skin graft and much intensive care from some burn unit, there wasn't much chance they would be useful in the bedroom ever again. It also served to make other punks ponder what the hell they were doing.

I would learn that all so-called pimps in the Bay Area, with Oakland and San Francisco in the lead, had come together, had some meeting and got the so-called pimps from the Bay all the way to Stockton and Sacramento to pool their money and put a contract out on my life. I had it on good authority so I knew it to be true. I didn't flinch. I declared war on pimps and punks and meant it. To the bone y'all, to the mothafuckinbone!!!

The Bay Area was so hot new laws were implemented. Add to that, we now had someone or some entity called "The Zodiac" straight on a tear all throughout the Bay Area. Moreover, we now had another situation that surfaced about the same time. They, the police and the media, called or dubbed "The Zebra Killers." This because they were reported to be all Black and their victims all white. Thus the name "Zebra."

It became law for some two years and some change that, if you were Black and lived in the Bay Area, you had to go to the DMV to get a special sticker for your vehicle and place it where "nab jones" could see it clearly. Plus, it was designed as to where it gave a sort of twinkle when hit up with any kind of light, more-so at night. If anyone Black was pulled over at night, claiming they were just getting off work, they had better have that sticker on their ride or else! Please believe it. Incidents between Blacks and police surfaced seemingly at an all-time high. The Bay was hotter than lava. My homies and I—especially Vic, who more often than not would go on missions with me—according to official reports flashed now and then, were responsible. Allegedly we had shot some **43** individuals (pimps and punks) y'all, pimps and punks!! We mopped[9] them dam near to Fresno. Only when the Bay became so hot and pigs began to ride three deep, and/ or with extremely large jet-black German shepherds, we had to hold it down. So we did. But we dam sho' weren't retired or finished. We had actually created a situation where, if you were Black, you could not be out after sun set in Oakland. This was the neo-official policy.

No matter what I did, I seemed to stay in trouble. There were some things constantly going down: shootings, railroads[10]—and we knew them to be just that—and in some cases clear-cut murder by the pigs. This was not just the case in Oakland but all over this country. It irked me, to say the least. The reasons for my seeming incessant in and out of jail was manifold. I have always loved my race, come what may. 'Til this day I strongly detest the way our youth carry themselves for the most part, minus a few. However, I love them just the same. Will always go down with them until such time Father Time renders me unable to. I'm just built like that. Straight from the gate.

I would catch another case in my late teens. My then girlfriend, a west side sister, and I were caught red-handed by her mother on the last day of the 12th grade having mad sex. Her mother, supposing to be at work, for whatever reason, came home early. There we were, asshole naked, doing the nasty. She pitched a fit, calling me every name in the book, and swore she was gonna have "the law" throw the book at me. She did just that. I would be arrested and charged with something called statutory rape (having sex with a girl under the age of 18 in California is a crime). They came and arrested me later that same night.

As a so-called ward of the state, I'm supposed to have certain rights. Shiiiittt. O.P.D. was like, "We know it's you been killing the homos, Jackson!" On and on they went. But I was like Sgt. Shultz on *Hogan's Heroes*—"I know nothing!!" Finally, when my day came around, sweet Rosalind up'ed and yelled at the judge, "He's my boyfriend!" And, despite the judge ordering her to remain seated and in control, she refused to be

---

[9] When fighting/murdering someone, they may produce an excessive amount of blood. *Source http://urbandictionary.com*

[10] To manipulate a situation such that events can only play out in a particular manner, or to a particular end, particularly in the case of a court trial. *Source http://urbandictionary.com.*

denied. She tossed her 2¢ in. No! Make that her 4¢! "I let him. You hear? I let him. He's my boyfriend. He didn't do nothing; I let him and will do it again." After some time lapsed, the judge had me stand. He firmly cautioned me about my behavior and if should we cross paths ever again. He then came with a new twist. He stated I "must either join the job corps or leave the Bay Area for five years." No two ways about it.

My father talked to me over and over. Then he got Huey and Mark Comfort to give it a shot. We sat around the dining room table and chopped it up. It was finally concluded I should join the army. In that way, I could travel. Get paid at the same time, and have sex galore, drink, smoke all the weed I wanted. And then there was Huey and Mark who talked to me even more outside the company of my father. "Brother," said Huey, "you can do reconnaissance for the party, brother. Finally do something constructive, brother. You can learn where and how to get weapons to be used against the very system that keeps trying to send you away or keep trying to off you. Work with me, brother. These young cats round here calling you 'Mad Dog.' I know. We have ears, brother. Come join the party. You used to hang with Lil Bobby, brother. He was your ace coon boon. This is a prime opportunity to really get some payback." That did it.

Shortly thereafter, I was at the induction center downtown. I exchanged info with the army rep. Everything went smooth as a baby's booty. When the time came, I took the aptitude test and passed with flying colors. They hooked me straight on up. Next thing you know, I was given a going away party. And boo-ya!! Off to Fort Polk, Louisiana I went. Daaamn skippy! I traveled abroad. Met many people in the (wrong) army. My two best potnas were from Fort Worth, Texas and the Bronx. Joe Wade, my boy from Fort Worth was just as sick as they come. He had a lot of me in him. Always looking to do dirt. And dirt we did. Plenty of it. My boy from the Bronx, David Johnson, well, let's just say he was a drinking and off-duty clubbing potna. Nowhere calculating and formidable like Joe.

So I would do a lil' stint in Sammy Sam's house. It was alright. Returned with all the cash, some savings bonds and had a gang of money I had sent to my mother and sister, of which they had not spent a penny. All of it was put up for safe keeping. That was how moms and sis rolled.

In the military, when chances allowed, I did foul shit. Laid a few down. Being there is no statute of limitation on murder, I will take Naughty by Nature's advice and "Guard my Grill!" Let's suffice it to say, I most certainly put a few heads to sleep. Like everywhere I ever went, it wasn't long before folks in the "service" came to learn that dude Jackson, he don't play fair. I even fucked off an E-7. [11]

        Eventually, it was time for me to go. I landed in Frisco International Airport, both feet on the ground running. My sister wouldn't let me ride home in the car with my father or the others that came to welcome me back home. I jumped in her SS Super Sport and slammed the door. "Boy! You gone break my window!" She fumbled with something. Then, from nowhere, I heard, "Pop that thang, bang bang!" I asked sis, "Who is that?" She looked at me bewildered and said, "That's the Isley Brothers, boy. Don't you know anythang?" We scratched out and hit the Golden Gate. In no time, I was back in Oakland. Official as official can get. I was back on the block. Had learned a lil some-some too.

---

[11] Sergeant First-Class in the Army.

Chapter 6
Prison

"Wanna see the scum of the Earth?
Watch the guards at San Quentin."
(Johnny Cash)
Live at San Quentin 1970

Perhaps there exist those who would say I am naught but a serial killer. Or, I am a psychopath. Perhaps a combination. I say without reservation: I am neither of the two. I have lived to witness firsthand a great number of people speak ill of my Comrade, Eldridge Cleaver—even Huey. "Eldridge, he running around raping women, forcing them to engage in acts of wild, unrestrained sex. All under the guise of what the white man did to us." A statement Huey delivered at Grove Street College yesteryear. My cousin recorded it and still harbors copies today, thus my source.

Regarding Eldridge, it would be only after he and I were cellies in Oakland CHJ (county jail), and I had the opportunity to truly listen to him, did I come to understand him. This was nothing like hearing him talk up on Shattuck and at the headquarters located in Oakland, or when he'd have folks' attention outside the Lamp Post nightclub. This was up close and personal and went deep into the wee, wee hours with no interval. Eldridge was certainly **not** a rapist. Notwithstanding, he forced himself on females time and again. Me, I understood him. His love for his people ran deeper than most. So much so he lashed out at the people who constantly lashed out at his own. He fought back in a different language. The language of violence. Call it what you will. Many seem to concern themselves with the irrefutable fact that Eldridge explained in great detail to each victim "why" he was about to do what he did. Perhaps, other than J.A. Rogers, Diop and maybe one or two other brother historians, he spotlighted a lil' something. Of those that had gone to college, of those who graduated with degrees of sort, how many have you ever heard speak about what the "white race" has done to us, and not just during slavery. I say that because we are still slaves, whether we like to hear it or not. We are! Eldridge knew this to be true, saw it to for what it actually was, and acted on it. So did I.

I am a revolutionary and nothing but. I partisan the concept of "revolutionary Black nationalism" and believe that slavery is yet in full effect. That there is and has been a war being waged against not just Black folk, but people of color the world over. Yes!! It is warriors and soldiers such as Eldridge Cleaver, my first cousin George Jackson, Fred Hampton, Alprentice "Bunchy" Carter, and I dare to mention the names of those in countries the world over who know these words to be true. Muslims in forefront. Now, as I write, sit-ins and protests are back with a new twist. Peoples—and not just our youth—elders are involving themselves with this new "occupying" philosophy. Seeds! Yet these people are actually fighting.

They, it will be argued by some, are non-violent—like King and Gandhi. Yet the fact remains, they are fighters against oppression, against any and all forms of capitalism, military occupation, genocide in form of economics, and the list goes on. Freedom fighter implies just that: someone or some people who deem they are not free and thus seek it. Was it not Comrade Assata who said, "People try to act like they don't know?"

I would go on record as saying I'm fond of the brother Al Sharpton. Brotherman has nuts. He don't merely speak to impress and let others witness he has gab. No! Al Sharpton tend to call a spade a spade. Jesse Jackson, in short, is full of it. History has always had a way of freeing up its secrets one way or another, long run or short run. Likewise, history has always produces those who seemingly have premonitions of some magnitude. I have always been one down to fight for my people, especially to fight and protect, and do what is warranted for my sisters. Pops instilled that in his sons. So, consequently, I took that with me wherever I have gone. It is then to be understood "why" I harbor complete ill-will toward so-called pimps. I make no bones about it: I shot many. After all, each time there were witnesses. Total difference when it comes to males who try to emulate females. Completely sickening. As far as I'm concerned, the CDC[12] in which I am being detained, these people are supposed to be about "rehabilitation"…some nerve. This very place, prison in California, allows males to receive panties in packages. Yes! They allow males to wear lipstick! High heeled pumps should not be far from approval at this rate. REHABILATATE? Man I tell ya. Sheer nerve.

Revolutionaries are cognizant of these types of "laws and rules." Muslims too. It appears to be the counterfeit Christians (those that follow the example of Jesus, a person who fought for what was right, for what was just, for people who have food to eat, he fought for people being oppressed) are not aware. Aside from those would-be Christians that stand—or more aptly HIDE—behind the pulpit, where are those who fight for what's right, and against oppression? Against people straight mobbing and taking other folks land, and assassinating their leaders and instilling they whom they deem should lead? Where are those people, those voices speaking out and physically doing something about the Earth's natural resources being depleted at an alarming rate? When will people stand up and question the

---

[12] California Department of Corrections

validity of those who claim Jesus was born in the month of December? Must I go on? These schemes—multi-billion and multi-trillion dollar schemes—are yet to be truly addressed. I don't intend to ramble; I intend to exhume; I intend to make manifest topics of concern. Intend to implore people to begin to inquire, to study the Unites States Constitution, learn it and learn it well. Indeed, just as **all** prophets were revolutionary, I've cast my lot in on their side. To take up the fight where they left off. As did Eldridge, George, Stokely, H. Rap and too many others just in my lifetime alone. And remember, I haven't even commended to spotlight the female freedom fighters—yet.

Every time you turn on your TV and some female is "missing," her husband is usually suspect. Or some child went missing, her mother or parents are suspect. Mothers killing their own offspring outright, drowning them, arson...again, need I go on? Let us not forget those in the religious circles, especially Catholic priests fondling boys of all ages. Many for a decade or better. Where's our voice? Justice? Proof of which: how much money have the Catholic shot-callers paid out in settlement, maybe say over the last decade? Man o' man. Sometimes just to be heard, one may have to subscribe to extreme deeds, but simultaneously be lettered. It then may well be a form of sacrifice.

Upon my return from the U.S Army, I began my association with true to form revolutionaries in earnest. I was constantly evolving. The 70s were kicking in. Revolutionary organizations were popping up some of everywhere. I was extended the opportunity to move in to what people in Oakland call "The Huey Newton Apartment." It is said to have been actually owned by the actress Jane Fonda, daughter of the actor Mr. Henry Fonda. Jane's associating with radicals, while traveling to Viet Nam, and her kicking it with my boy Huey was well known. This apparently took place while I was in the Army. In any event, I moved into the Huey Newton High Rise on the top floor. There, I met revolutionaries galore. The entire building was occupied by nothing but militants and activists of all sort.

On the floor I stayed lived the soon to be known Donald "Cinque" Defreeze; the brother who kidnapped Patty Hearst! He immediately took a liking to me, and we began our association. Cinque, as we called him and as he preferred, loved singer Marvin Gaye. He fancied himself after Marv, especially the kufi cap, his facial hair and dress code. Like Huey, Eldridge and George, Cinque had that gift of gab. All the more-so when he was high on weed.

Through Cinque, I would meet Brother-comrade Earl Satcher. Earl was simply called "Black Buddha." He was Comrade George's martial arts teacher in prison. Black Buddha was cut like a bomb-ass sculpture by one with the surest hands. He had a raw "Fu-Man Chu" mustache and he, like the others, most certainly had that gift of gab. Worked out every single day and implored me to do likewise. Sometimes I did, other times—naw. Buddha would start an entity that became known as The Tribal Thumb. They, in time, would birth the radical S.L.A. (Symbionese Liberation Army) from the mind of Cinque and my boy Cecil Moody.

Unlike the Tribal Thumb, which consisted of absolutely nothing but females, Earl (Black Buddha) was the only male. Aside from himself, he didn't believe in working or struggling with other males. He would be the sole male and shot caller, come what may. And so that's how the Tribal Thumb got down: Earl calling the shots, all white girls—and white girls only. They specialized in robbing banks and robbing banks only. Berkeley is where they hung their hats.

Often, Black Buddha, Cinque and I would sit around eating pumpkin seeds and watching Cinque's ants. He had an extraordinarily large fish tank that he converted into a home and colony for ants he brought back from a trip down to Texas. These ants were very aggressive, and anything we caught and dropped in the tank, the ants would rush in and dismember it in no time. It became almost a habit for us to smoke weed, bump some Marvin or Funkadelic, and watch the ants do their thing.

It would be situations just mentioned when Buddha would stop by with white girls. Sometimes one, sometimes two. We would smoke weed with them, talk about the events of the day and time—especially Nixon— and we would chat about people in the struggle abroad. Most of the females Buddha brought over the Cinque's and my apartment were attending U.C. Berkeley. Such is how I met Patricia Hearst. Buddha brought her and a friend by, we smoked weed, talked about the world.

Buddha cut[13] Patty into Cinque long before the misadventures of the S.L.A. and all this junk about Patty was kidnapped. I know for a fact, first

---

[13] To combine, as in to cut drugs. *http://urbandictionary.com*

hand, that all this was a well-thought out plan and, later, Cinque confided in me that it was in fact Patty's idea to kidnap her father for money. He told me of how she just plain hated her father. He was said to be a stone-cold racist. It was Patty who brought the idea to Cinque. There were numerous times her and her friend would come over, drop acid or smoke weed mixed with hash. And, Cinque would pull Patty into the bedroom and they would go at it. Loud, mad sexxx. I never got with her friend because white girls just don't do nothing for me, notwithstanding I had more sisters than I could ever possible service. They were there many times when these honkey bitches—the sisters would call them—came by. Patty was absolutely crazy over Cinque. He told me all about her. Her love for Black meat, as he described it. Patty loved Sly and the Family Stone, and I'd bump her favorite for her when they were at my apartment. "There's a Riot Going On!" Patty Hearst had a connection in Berkeley and she would often bring with her or already be high on acid. White girls were ultra-notorious for "acid trips and skinny dips" at the Berkeley Marina. Patty used to talk about it brazenly, and would often take issue with me for not getting with her friend. Truth be told, baby girl had a weird body odor! Perhaps this was why they also would sometimes bring different types of incense, some of which was straight bomb though!

Once, while messing around, I accidentally spilled a little hot wax from a candle on Patty's left foot. Ever since then she seemed to dislike me, as if she somehow thought I did it on purpose. It was a pure accident, and in fact, was not even that serious. What was, was when Cinque told me she might be pregnant. I was like daaaamn!!!

In addition to meeting Patty Hearst and witnessing her buck wild sexcapades with Cinque, I also met other members of the S.L.A., but that happened a bit later. I met and became close potnas with Russ Little. He taught me coding and some demolition skills. I met Joe Romero, a Hispanic, somewhat temperamental and just returned from Viet Nam. I met brother Cecil Moody, the only other brother (or Black) aside from Cinque himself. Cecil was vicious with the martial arts and one time, while we were in Oakland County Jail together, he musta' whooped like four or five police before they finally got him on the ground. Of course I would have helped, but this took place outside the B-tank cells where there were bars between us. Cecil told me of their S.L.A. plans to bomb Laney College during a football game to get media attention. They did in fact plant a bomb, but it was discovered before it detonated. I last saw Cecil Moody in the C.H.J. in Oakland, just when they were forming the S.L.A. We were tight and practiced the arts together.

I was also cell mates with both Russ Little and Joe Romero in Oakland's county jail when they decided to try to escape. They invited me, but I told them it was too risky; they hadn't been there long enough to learn the lay of the land, so to speak. It was too spontaneous despite them wanting to get a move on before trial concluded and they were shipped off the pen. So, they made an attempt. They overpowered the guards and managed to make it to the armory, but, what they didn't know was that each key was made to turn only so far, and either to the left or to the right. Also, they learned—the hard way I might add—the phones in Oakland's courthouse jail were rigged to where if they were off the hook for three seconds, they automatically set off an alarm. The S.L.A. members never had a chance. They were done before they even got started.

While in C.H.J., I kept the wolves at bay. Many brothers wanted to straight down the S.L.A. members there for the assassination of then school superintendent, Marcus Foster, which stayed on TV for the longest. This political assassination was followed by the would-be, so-called kidnapping of Patricia Hearst (Miss Acid Head!). During the time at the Huey Newton High Rise, when Patty was around, she often seemed to be spoiled, and a snob. Wanted everything her way, and would become loud if it didn't go her way. Me, I could care less if she had money or not, I'd tell Cinque. I really and truly engaged them to the extent that I did strictly for the weed, acid and hash when they had it. Other than that, I was cool on her and her flat-assed friend.

I recall while in the Oakland County Jail, Brother-comrade Black Buddha came through. This was just two or three months before they were caught and the "Shootout with S.W.A.T." down in southern California. Buddha and I watched as the pigs took Cinque and company out. When all the media reports started to filter in, they spoke at length with regards to Patty being kidnapped. Buddha and I looked at each other and was like, "KIDNAPPED?!" They need to quit it. Never did it ever surface that Patty was the sole author of the entire script. It was her who strongly disliked her father. So much so she joined ranks with revolutionaries to kidnap him. Cinque was said to have knocked Patty up. Patty's father got wind of it and threatened to stall Patty out of the will and a whole bunch of other noise because of the clout he had, so Lil' Miss Acid Head becomes disgruntled, gets the abortion and thus hates dear old dad forever more.

We also heard it from the S.L.A. comrades direct—as we could stay up late and kick it—about how they obtained very valuable information from Patty. Such is how they were able to feign like they would release Patty if her father would give one million dollars in food away to the poor and needy there in Oakland, which he did. But, what the masses didn't know was that while everyone was focused on the free one million dollar food give-away, Patricia had provided the S.L.A. with information regarding some secret papers being kept in a Rockefeller Building in New York. The papers, according to Miss Acid Head, were about a certain specific Black presidents of the United States of America that had passed for white, their lineage, which masonic lodge they attended and more.

The million dollar free food give-away, in truth, was a diversion. Two S.L.A. members had crept to New York, armed with the information provided by Patty, which proved to be valid and accurate, as the S.L.A. members were successful in liberating said papers. Then, contact was established with Patty's father and an arrangement reached with regard to having the papers made public. Patty's father agreed, and did so under one condition (so we were told, but on very good authority). The one condition was that he, Patty's father, at the suggestion of the F.B.I. whom convinced him to publish the papers but to do so under the title "Mumble Jumble." The S.L.A. agreed with this and the papers were published. I know this to be true because I received a copy right there in Oakland County Jail, where I read the book "Mumble, Jumble" myself. And, apparently, the F.B.I.'s advice to Mr. Hearst proved beneficial because very few people to this very day even know about the book, and this is primarily because of the title given to it: Mumble Jumble. People tend to walk right on by it at book stores, etc., without giving it a second glance.

Brother-comrade Azikiwe Kambon and I read it individually and then together. We then discussed it a length. We also made brothers aware that came through the county jail during the two years and seven months I was there and Azikiwe just about the same, fighting murders. There was no détente reached between the S.L.A. and Patty's father. This actually explains why she was not "released" after the million in food give-away.

Chapter 7

Declaration

(The World's 1st Communist Muslim Socialist)

"In every person exists three entities:
THE PUBLIC SELF
THE PRIVATE SELF
THE REAL SELF."
         (Sun Tzu)

It is truly amazing what money can do. I have already been made aware that the "mighty Hearst" clan will not be beholding to this particular chapter of my book. Personally, I couldn't care one way or the other. I was never fond of Patty or whitegirls any-dam-way, so exert your power, Hearsts. I can only die once, but the truth will live forever.

Folks running round here blaming a brother for so-called brainwashing this Jezebel, acid-head Patty. Fat chance. If people were employing common sense, then why didn't absolutely any of the public find it in the least bit strange: a female (Patty), with a machine gun fully loaded, with a banana clip no less? In a car by herself (Patty was), why didn't she just drive right on to the Golden Gate right there, or just drive to any gas station or until she saw a cop? Why didn't she endeavor to get away, even in a car all by her lonesome, with a machine gun and a full banana clip? But nope! She follows them into the bank. Gets a shot off, remember? So, the machine gun was no fake. It worked like a mini-skirt, as the Panthers used to say. Then, she gets back into the car, all by her lonesome mind you, and does what? Follows the first car hither and yon. Knock it off, Patty. You're no better than the flat-assed Jezebel who made up the story yester-year on the Scottsboro boys. Then, later, after her conscious ate her lying flat-ass alive, she fessed-up. "I made it all up. They never touched me. They never laid a hand on me." Fine, she came clean, one might say, but she did that shit after they had already served time. Yeah, how foul is that? Anybody ever wonder why movie making folks like Spike Lee and Tyler Perry won't touch stories like this? They have not the heart to make a movie about lying-ass, flat-assed Patty Hearst. A BLACK version!! Randy Hearst, even dwelling six-feet deep, retains too much clout, and brothers retain too much fear. We will make them bunk-ass movies about a comedic Black grandmother and what not. Something with absolutely no academic enlightenment attached. Yet, Spike Lee and others I heard with my own two ears, talk that shit about 50Cent and other rappers wearing bullet-proof vests and/ or they have their sons, etc., wearing a bullet-proof vest and is naught but a child. When, truth be told, IT'S'FUCKED UP FOR US TO HAVE TO WEAR ANYTHING BULLET-PROOF ANYTIME, ANYWHERE. Hell, we ain't in Iraq, Afghanistan someplace. Yo! Spike Lee, speak on that!!!!! Aye, Tyler, you got that Georgia Peach hook-up; a self-ran studio. How's about you tackling the above for a movie AND keep it real? Yeah. That's what I thought...

You guys will do some watered down bullshit about the Panthers, the Nation of Islam and Malcolm [X], but scared out of ya lil' bloomers to tackle something such as how Randy [Hearst] played us. And, let us tell it, we got a meal-ticket of free food. To quote Kris Kross, "We missed the bus!" I'm here for the rest of my life and I ain't tripping. One thing you can bet about me: come whatever, whenever and however, I'm real as they come. I don't squat to pee. Believe the hype!!!

Living amongst radicals at the Huey Newton Hi-rise proved to be a lifestyle changing experience. It would be while staying there my outlook about worldly affairs would be altered—forever. From there I would leave California and travel across this stolen soil, meeting radical Indians along the way, become acquainted with the Weather Underground, and it would be from living at this apartment building that my oldest son would be conceived. It would also be at this self-same apartment that I myself would be robbed. Yes, me:the "Robin Hood" of Northern California.

When I moved into the Huey Hi-Rise, I also packed up and took my beautiful black and chrome drum set, a Ludwig model. It was totally ok and no one ever complained. I had four large three-foot speakers and some eight smaller ones hooked up throughout the apartment. I had more albums than the law allows. At this time there were only albums and 8-tracks, of which I had plenty of each. I would often toss on a James Brown LP...*There Was a Time* was one of my favorites to play to. *Cold Sweat* was the other. I'd play them over and over and over until I got the drumbeat down pat.

One time while playing the drums to an album, my door buzzed. I went and checked it out. It was a guy I'd never seen before. He introduced himself as "Juan." He was Puerto Rican and claimed to be from New York. He inquired: "Do I be hearing a live band or something coming from your place, man?" To which I replied, "Naw. I just gotta drum set and be playing sometimes. I also got some keyboards I hit up every now and then. What's up? I'm disturbin' you or something?" He replied in the negative and told me that he in fact played the guitar. That started the socializing. I invited him in, introduced him to my then pregnant girlfriend, El, and he took a seat. We chopped it up. I asked him did he smoke weed and he was sho'nuff wit it. So much so he added, "I got some too. Umma go get a lil' and you can smoke a joint of mine and I'll smoke a joint of yours." So, we did. It was cool. Juan and I hit it right off. Everything seemed rippy-dippy.

After a period of time went by, Juan started buying weed from me. Nothing major, just small shit. Later still, he would introduce me to one of his potnas; a frail white dude. Said his name was Marshal. We chatted, drank a lil' bit, made the weed transaction and the two of them departed. This went on for a lil' bit. There would come a time when Marshal started coming by without Juan—and unannounced. He had money and I needed it, so I didn't too much trip. Long as he was spending loot.

One particular time, Marshal came by without Juan, but with another 'wood I'd never seen before. When they hit the buzzer for me to buzz them up, I didn't think anything of it. Thinking they was going to be business as usual. I buzzed them up. When they made it to the top floor and hit my door, I looked out and it was Marshal and some other cat. Still, I didn't trip. I let them in. Walked them into my living room, offered them a seat and asked politely, "What you guys want?" The bigger of the two—the new 'wood—stood up and pulled out a foe-five mag (.45mm), pointed it at me, and said, "We want all ya' dope, kneegar!" I told dude, "A, all bullshit aside, don't point ya' roscoe at me, man. I done had hella homies get shot like that on'ah humbug." He advanced towards me and said, "Gimme all ya' dope, kneegar, or I'll keel ya' ass." I sat back in my Addams Family chair that Huey had given me, looked at this cat and said to him, "You trippin' man. Listen, if y'all want a lil' weed, I can..." That was it. That's all I can remember. When I regained consciousness, my girl was on her knees holding a bloody towel up to my forehead. I had been hit by his .45 and it ruptured a blood vessel. My girl, pregnant and starting to show, nose was bleeding, right eye was closed and bleeding from the mouth as well. Vic, he was alive and well. They did not touch him for some reason. Just issued threats, and he ran them all down to me.

"We want all ya' dope, kneegar. All of your dope connections, too. We know who he is, and if he don't give you all his dope to give to us, we gonna keel all you kneegars. We'll be back tomorrow at 4 o' clock!" I almost couldn't believe it. El, she was outright hysterical. "They gonna kill us. You gonna get me killed, Mike." On and on she went. Then she dropped her bomb: "I'm leaving. I'm gonna call James (her brother) and have him come get me." And she did just that. Consequently, I was in this giant penthouse apartment all by myself. Later I got Vic to drive me to my big homies spot in the deep east. King Dee! He was actually older than I but knew me, and knew my brothers as well. Dee gave me action at grinding weed for him, with plenty enough for me to smoke at random on the side. So it was. I rang his door bell. When his girl, Mattie, came to the door and saw me, blood all over my lime-green silk tee shirt, lime-green corduroy jeans and desert boots, she tripped. "Dee!" she yelled over her shoulder. "Come here. Hurry up, it's Michael."

Big homie, King Dee, as we call him, appeared, peeped me and inquired as to what happened. I started in: "You know that quarter pound I got from you? Well, some whiteboys robbed me man. One of um hit me with his gun. They 'round here talkin' 'bout they know who you is, and they want all ya' dope or they gone kill you and me both. They said they want it by 4 o' clock tomorrow or we dead, man." King Dee assured me they were wolfing. He instructed Sister Mattie to look out for me. I never went to a hospital. She hooked me up. She cleaned my wound, put iodine on it, and then covered it with two gauze pads and tape. Back on the block. Vengeance would be mine if the two that did this to me and I ever crossed paths again. Count on it.

Dee let me slide with regard to the quarter pound I'd got from him on credit. I jumped back in my ride, hit the McArthur freeway, headed back to the crib on the Northside; the Hi-rise.

Lonely be the word. My girl was gone, Vic was at home and there I was in this giant penthouse all alone. I commence to straighten things up from where they had ransacked the place. The only thing they took was my weed, hidden in a White Owl cigar box, all four of my 3-foot speakers and the cash I had in the cigar box; approximately $200.00. My mind was racing a mile a minute. I began to entertain thoughts of offin' Juan. After all, it was he had introduced us. He set me up. Blast him on sight is how I was tripping, when, all of a sudden, there was a knock on the door. Not the buzzer way down stairs, but my door. Someone was in the hall. Someone had made their way to my very door. I wasn't—and seemed to could not—thinking straight. A lot had happened that rubbed me the wrong way that day. My girl, pregnant with my child, whooped on by some woodchuck, in my place. MY PLACE. No! It was not supposed to go like that—never, ever. Something in me guided me to the door and I opened it without even so much as asking, "Who is it?"

There, standing before me was a 'hippie' looking brother. Full beard. About six feet. Same complexion as me. Smoking a corn pipe. He smiled easily and said, "Hey brother, my wife was in the kitchen and, you know, your window faces ours, and she said she seen two ofays in your apartment and they was brandishing weapons, and we were just wondering if you were alright?" I tore into him verbally: "Man, look at my forehead!" I said to him, "Them chucks robbed me man. Beat my broad down too. They took all my weed except this I had on me. Wanna smoke a joint?"

The brother stood very erect, never taking his eyes off of me. He rubbed his beard and said to me, "Brother, aren't you related to George Jackson?" I looked at him closely trying to detect any sign of danger now. I threw caution to the wind. I said, "Yeah. Why?" The brother told me, "Brother, you hail from a family of soldiers. Revolutionaries. Your family has a unique history. You are the youngest. Your slave name is Michael, isn't it?" "Slave name?" I said. He said, "Mm hmm. That's what it is. And here it is, you have a sister pregnant, and you are selling drugs, and having people in and out of your place at all hours. Sometimes we can smell the weed all out in the hall." Till this point, I had never seen this dude before and most certainly had no idea he lived on the exact same floor. I only knew Cinque. That was it. The brother said to me, "Brother, will you excuse me for a minute? I want to go and get somebody. I'll be right back."

Shownuff, in about two or three minutes, he reappeared with some brother, very short and also sporting a full beard, a kufi cap, and puffing on a corn pipe. They mumbled something to each other, looked at me, and asked, "Can we come in?" I've heard it said the God works in mysterious ways. Perhaps that is what this was: intervention from a higher authority. I had totally let my guard down. They could've been related to someone I had blasted—or worse. I stepped back in such a manner so as to allow them to enter. And they did.

Inside I closed the door and followed them into my living room. I offered them weed, which they vehemently refused and scolded me for engaging in such activity after what went down in my apartment just a short time ago. Truth be told, I wasn't tryin' to hear it. I got me some zag from my dresser drawer, strolled back to the living room and threw on some music. One of them, the shorter of the two (whom for now we will refer to as "Shorty") asked me if I could turn it off, stating that we needed to talk. No big thang. I turned the music off. But, my instincts told me it was something different about these two dudes. Very, very different. I didn't feel threatened at any time, nor was I in fear of them. I somehow knew: Relax. Call it what you will, but somehow I knew I was going to be alright.

I explained to Shorty exactly what I had told his potna, leaving nothing out. These two brothers stayed in my apartment until very late. Perhaps one o'clock in the morning, give or take. They took great pains to explain unto me that it was not Juan who had set me up, but in fact and truth, it was myself. Anytime you tell anyone "I have some dope for sale," you right then and there just snitched on yourself. Whatever occurs as a result happened because you yourself first told on yourself. Anything and everything that jumped off afterward did so because of my opening my mouth in the first place. It was very clear and I understood. From that point on, I never sold dope again. My instincts told me this was the genesis of something long lacking in my life. I somehow knew to pay attention and take heed.

After a while, the two stood up to leave. They assured me that they would be back tomorrow before the 4 P.M. deadline given by the woodchucks. They slipped out the door and I put on some music, fixed up a joint kicked back and thought about what all had taken place that day. I wasn't afraid, yet I slept with my antenna sky high and one eye open. Night turned into morning. Morning into noon and soon, evening was fighting its way in. Vic, the brother I embraced as my best friend, was nowhere to be found. My girl, El, I could readily understand her position. So I was like, well, they didn't find my .22 when they ransacked my apartment. Still got that. If the woods show, let the chips fall where they may. I was duty bound to stand my ground. It wasn't even in me to do otherwise. I bumped music and passed the day away doing much of nothing. Around 2 P.M., there was a knock at my door. It was the hippie looking brothers. I open the door and they came in and greeted me warmly, stating, "Brother, don't worry. Everything gonna be alright." To which I responded, "I ain't even trippin', nigga." One of the two, the short one, must'ah hurried up and check me. "Listen, brother. There are no 'niggers' in here and we'd highly appreciate if you not use that word. Also refrains from using it out of our company." I tripped. In particular, the way the brothers spoke. No slang. They didn't smoke weed (free weed in Oakland...unheard of). They didn't drink. And, every time one of them spoke, it as with absolute clarity and directly to the point. I honored their request. Right about that time, my door buzzes. It was Victor. I was glad to see him. I knew he wouldn't let me down. I introduced him to the brothers. As they exchanged pleasantries, in a flash, they chewed him out just as they did me about using the N-word. Vic got the message and it wasn't heard anymore from that point on.

Wasn't' long before 3 o'clock rolled around and the two hippie looking brothers got up to leave. They said on their way out, "Brother, just know, we'll be back, and we have our eyes on your place." With that, they slipped out the door. Immediately, Vic and I started making preparations to get high. We came to the conclusion that if the two ofays actually did come back, we was either gonna be in the county jail or the county morgue. And, in either case, we were gonna be as loaded as possible if and when the time came. We smoked the weed I had left. Finished it off and shifted from one conversation to the next. Vic was totally convinced they wouldn't dare come back. It was enough for two ofays to rob a brother in—what?—82% Black Oakland? Yet we also recognized they had the hearts of gunslingers to do the shit they did.

Just as stated, the two brothers reappeared at my door about a half hour after they left. Only, this time, they both had on full body length black leather coats. They came in, cool as a summer breeze. I offered seats unto them, but they sternly refused. Suddenly, my door buzzes. Silence covered the entire apartment. I go my box and inquire, "Who is it?" "It's me!" a voice replied. My baby had come back. Yeah, maybe, just maybe, things were taking a turn for the better. I must'ah hurried up and let her in. In fact, I ran down all those flights of stairs and met her. She had her brothers James and David with her. We were never tight and had nothing in common except that their sister and I were a couple. Pregnant now, I was there to stay, like it or not. I talk to the two of them and was successful in convincing them that I would give her a ride back. Reluctantly, they left.

Inside, I introduced El unto the two brothers. When she walked into the living room, even before I introduced everybody, her entire facial expression changed drastically. I could see she didn't want to be there. I was of the opinion, if she really didn't want to be there, she sure had bad timing, knowing the two ofays said they would return at 4pm, and it was just about that on the nose. And, shonuff, right about then, I hear a buzz. Once again, complete silence fell over the entire apartment. Everybody stared at everybody. So, off to the box I go. I inquired into the speaker box, "Who is it?" I heard a reply; "Open the door, kneegar." I all but couldn't believe it. The two hippie looking brothers said, "Just let them in, brother.

Don't do nothing else, just let them in. We'll handle it from there." I hit the buzzer. Shortly, my door is pounded on. Mistake #1: the ofays had the nerve to actually come back. When I opened the door, it was only one of the two. The smaller of the two. Not the one who had hit me. Mistake #2: he came into the apartment instead of requesting me to go get the dope and bring it to him at the door. No! Instead, in total and complete disregard of where he was, and with absolute confidence that his kneegar had been broken, he strolled down my long hallway, and said over his shoulder as he looked at the albums, posters and strobe lights I had hooked up, "Git my dope, kneegar." I feigned properly, "I ain't got it right here, man. I just don't want no trouble. I got some 151. Wanna drink?" He said sarcastic as humanly possible, "Do it look like I wanna drink, kneegar?" At that point, Shorty burst out of my closet with a foe-five mag in hand, dropped to one knee in a completely professional manner, aiming the foe-five directly at the ofay. Then, the second brother appeared from around the side of my dining room via the kitchen, catching the ofay completely by surprise. I then made him sit on my sofa, came and squatted directly in front of him, looked him right in his honkey-blue eyes and said, "I know you told all your buddies about how you guys robbed and pistol whipped a nigga, huh?" He swallowed extremely hard and tried to look off. I grabbed his face and jerked it back around with so much force his gun fell out. Daammmm, dude was strapped all the time and I wasn't even aware. I musta' hurried up and grabbed his roscoe then stood up. I hit him as hard as I could right in the face with it. He fell back on my couch and screamed. Here comes El out the bedroom, screaming at the top of her lungs. Shorty looked sternly at me and told me, "Brother, control your woman!" I froze for a hot second, got my wits about me and advanced towards her. I took her by the forearm and led her back into our bedroom, closed the door behind us and told her, "Listen, baby. Just stay in here and look at some t.v. Just don't come back out; stay here." Having said that, I stormed back into my living room and straight at the 'wood, like a bee to honey. Beat him with no mercy whatsoever. Then it occurred to me: throw this muthafucka out da picture window and watch him all the way down. Fuckit! I grabbed dude, beat him even more. Knocked him unconscious. Him, not even worthy of having my water tossed on him to revive him so that I might whoop on that ass some more. Naw! Hell naw!! I just waited until he came around on his own volition. In the mean and in between, the two brothers said unto me, "Listen brother, be cool. Go and be with your girl. We are going to take this ofay on a gangsta ride. We're going to wait until its dark, then we'll go down the backstairs." Sounded like a plan to me. And that's exactly what we did. As soon as the sun declined, we were on the move. Out the door and down the back we went. Once on the ground floor, we peeped out front, it was all good with the exception of it not being all good for the 'wood. For him it was straight curtains. We shoved him in the trunk of my ride, all four of us: Vic, the two hippy-looking brothers, and me at the wheel, cut it out. We took ol' boy up in the hills. Got him out my trunk and, with no words whatsoever, I put my own gun, the one they had used to pistol whoop me and rupture an artery, yea, that gun, yea, I damsho did, put it up to his temple and squeezed.

I then jumped back in my car and took off. Then, all of a sudden, something within me told me to freeze, go back. I put my car in reverse. One of the brother's said, "What are you doing, brother?" I didn't even speak, I just went on with what I had in mind. Back on the scene, I hopped out, went back to the ole ofay, and put two more in his head. Then said, "Seven-tray every gotdam day!" and was outtie. The brothers looked at me and asked me, "What was that all about, brother?" I told them, "I'm from the seven-tray, man. That's our hood; 73rd Ave. We call it the tray for short. Seventy-third or seven-tray. Us do-or-die muthafuckas on the east side of the Bay." I went on for a bit as I drove back to my apartment. "Our hood, they call us down and dirty, brah. 'Cause we gets down and we don't believe in fighting fair. We fight what some call "dirty!" Down and dirty, that be we. We don't give 'ah fuck, man. Never have, never will." They said nothing else all the way back to the apartment building

Once back, we chatted for a second. They said, "Whatever you do brother, you and your friend are not to tell anyone about what just took place." I assured them that we wouldn't. They went up the back way. Vic and I, the front. When we reached my apartment and stepped in, blam. There was El. Standing there with her arms folded, alongside my father. I said, "What's up, Pops?" My father looked right in my eyes and said, "Boy! What you done did?" "Nothing, Pops. Just got into a fight with this honkey, that's all." He asked me, "Is that why you got that pad over your eye?" I said, "Yeah! Ain't no big thang. Lil' fight, that's all." He then reached into the side pocket of his coat and tossed a little wallet on the table; my coffee table. It was the ofay's. It had fallen out when I was on that ass and once we were gone (taking him on that ride), El found it, called my father and he came right over. The next day, it was on the news. A "taxi cab driver" found outta here like last year. Finished. Through. Never to ever hit or whip on another kneegar. Best believe that!!!

From that point on, my association with the two hippy-looking brothers intensified so, it is hard to believe. I stopped hangin' with Vic'nem. I severed ties with all the people I knew on this planet, minus El. Either in their apartment or mine, I'd spend the entire day and night. Looking at various newspapers they had Black folk at odd with whites. Sisters being dragged off by pigs with their panties showing. Brothers being viciously bit by pig-dogs. Real, real vicious beatings, not just the ones of my race being hit by the immense-pressure water hoses. No! That was commonplace. I mean these brothers had papers and photos nowhere near the norm. I had seen Nation of Islam newspaper, Muhammad Speaks and Black Panther Newspaper time and again, even sold a few here and there with my sojourn with the Panthers. No! The papers to which I refer, I had never seen nor heard of before. The most radical ever. They put papers like Burning Spear and all such peers to utter shame. I reviewed papers for days on end. Shortly, those days turned into weeks. In time, we became inseparable. This was my genesis, so to speak. My so-called homeboys would come by and I was distant. I didn't care to associate any longer, as I was totally familiar with what they cared to talk about. Money, sex and getting high; absolutely nothing about helping their people on any level. Me, I was now beginning to understand that which I had learned up to that point in my life. After some time, months, I was invited to go on "survival missions" with the two brothers. During such, I learned how to secure weapons from the enemy camp, especially those with rifles in the cab of their truck, and or those out hunting. I also learned from the two brothers how to extract various poisons from the SPCA's[14] and learned more about the demolition concerns than I did when I was Sam's Army. With my two new potnas, I learned about "fasting" and eating of nothing but chocolate which ensues with puritanical bursts of energy. I learned "not" to shoot animals for fun and game but only if directly related to survival. Although I knew about protecting our sisters/ females, some of what I knew was twisted. My brothers straightened it all out in time. I learned in full the accurate concept of right wing philosophy, how to detect racists, about restraint, when and when not to expose my hand. I was made cognizant of the five

---

[14] Society for the Promotion of the Communist Agenda

major people and also about their cultures. Blacks, who in truth are NOT!--they are African. The origin of the word Africa is Roman, the continent being renamed after the war of Zama between Rome and one of our famous, serious as they come homies, Hannibal. This Roman general, Syprocil, or Sipricol Africanus, beheaded Hannibal's older brother, Hasdrubal. He was also successful in capturing Hannibal's mother, to which he sent word to Hannibal, who was at that time knocking on the doors of Rome. Or I should say knocking on the walls of Rome. Upon receiving this information, Hannibal capitulated. The Romans went wild. So much so, they renamed the continent after this Roman general, Sipricol Africanus. The continent became known as Africa. The war of Zama took place a bit over 4,000 years ago.

I learned about the brown race, the red race, the yellow and the white. The Red Indian, our true brothers, should have absolutely no beef with our people. As for the yellow and brown, (Chinese and Japanese), it is the same truth. There should be no beef. My race has not wronged these people or their race. It is not nor has it ever been my race who introduced any disease of any sort, biological weapons, nor dropped atomic bombs. Twice on the same people; the Japanese. This wasn't Blacks that did that. It was not my kith and kin who introduced alcohol, disease of sort, and genocide unto the Indians. It wasn't the African, if you will, who smashed on India. It was not my race, Blacks, who straight moved on the Chinese, the Korean and introduced drugs of all sort, especially drugs derived from the poppy plant. Is it who you know not, dear reader?

In any event, I was learning. In absolutely no time, I gained complete control over self. I reflected back to the things I'd learned from Huey and Eldridge and numerous others. Those things began to take on a new form in terms of clarity. We often went on these get-aways. We traveled to various state forests and engaged in target practice. This enhanced our knowledge of weaponry and how to utilize such. I learned the true meaning of Darwin's philosophy of survival of the fittest, which, in truth, means every man for himself!

Time rolled on. In time, I'd be allowed inside the ultra-secret world of these two brothers. The one referred to herein as Shorty, come to find out, was a "mathematician" and had in fact snuck all the way inside communist Red China and back. Boy did I learn from him. The best, uncontested mentor I've ever came across in my entire lifetime, bar none.

His ability to interpret and calculate accurately would astound you. Little did I know, but was soon to find out, I had become annexed with so called number 2 and number 8 on the FBI's 10 Most Wanted List.

I would in time, be given a cultural name, and Eleanor would also be gave a name; Jamilah. The brothers would mostly call me "Ja-Ja," which means A MAN WHO STICKS TO WHAT HE BELIEVES IN. Me, I loved it. They asked me if I would consider leaving California with them. I was absolutely elated. Couldn't wait. I saw Cinque, Hue, my so-called homeboys, my family and others a few more times. We set a time to depart and everything we did was centered around our leaving California. I sold my car when the time was right, then doubled back and laid that individual down that I had sold it to. We hit a major lick in 'Frisco. Got 63 grand out of it too. We then bought a bomb truck. Put work into it. Put various hidden compartments into it. Made need-be arrangements with Jamilah on exactly what was taking place and that I would never forsake or turn my back on her and my child. With that, we left California, pulling a U-Haul trailer we rented for the occasion. Regarding it, we labored hard on it to attain our desires. In the end, the U-Haul was fixed where it could contain all of the weapons we had….or *they* had when I met and got to know them. A cache of weapons including a crate of 50 hand grenades. Because of the courage I displayed once in the south Bay, I was allowed to do something special. I was actually allowed to give a hand grenade to one of my real potnas who later became a fully functioning member of the BGF. Jewel Harrison, aka "STANK!" I grew up with Stank. He had also rode with us directly on the pigs numerous times back in our youth heyday. I gave Stank a hand grenade up at Quick Ways on East 14th, right out of the trunk of my car. He hugged me then, and some 11 years later, he hugged me again, only this time inside San Quentin. Later still, we were in Folsom together. Ole Stank—wonder whatever became of him, and others. So, I had embraced a new name, new ideology, and new objective in life. I was now a fully functioning member of the Black Liberation Army. And one thing, I was not hardly bullshitting.

Travelling with the military wing of the "B.L.A., I met with numerous people that were out and about to "bring ameriKKKa to its knees." I was introduced to some people of European descent, called themselves "The Weather Underground" and/ or just plain Weathermen. Some preferred not to be addressed as Weathermen because they had female comrades too. I met members of the Brown Berets. Some of the most impressive and clandestinely organized were the radical Indians who my newfound comrades knew and thus allowed us to travel and rest on their land. They treated us with so much respect. We travelled across this stolen land of ameriKKKa, and was allowed to take refuge on Indian reservations. I also was fortunate enough to meet and...do some things...with my Comrade Kuwasi Balagoon (rip) on the east coast. I would experience living in a safe house with various other comrades such as Assata Shakur, Fulani Ali, Julassi Sadiqqui, and Sister-comrade Iyana—she and Julassi helped me understand a great number of things. Like, why we communicated face-to-face. Or, why our military wing did not employ the so-called service of mail. No letters would be sent unto any 'rade. Anything and everything had to be conducted face-to-face. They helped me to understand "why" the adults ate first and the children second. Simply because the adults were charged with discharging the responsibilities of making sure all was safe. We would always continue to be. As be the case in nature. Thus we are forever reminded in both al-Quran and the Bible to "study nature!"

While on the move to show and prove, we happened upon some right wingers in the colony of Utah. As we rode towards the colony of Colorado, a jeep passed us. Clearly, we saw them peep us. Looking back, we saw their red brake lights, and then they busted a "U." We knew what time it was. I has heard much and was well prepared for whoever if we chanced upon someone or some people tripping that racial bullshit. As it were, they were. The jeep sped up and soon was side by side with our International Truck. We had organized ourselves where one of the three of us would always be in the back of the U-Haul, fully armed to the "t." More often than not, I was riding in the back, Comrade Louis (of course that was not his real name) was the designated driver. Shorty rode shotgun with the .45 on his person. If they wanted that funk, they'd get it.

They blew the horn, shouted, and the one riding shotgun made motions for us to pull over. At this point, I was in the [bed of] the U-Haul; completely off the radar. It became obvious they were not going to go away, so Louis pulled over. Immediately, the two jumped out of their jeep and hurried towards the truck, paying no mind to the U-Haul whatsoever. They approached the truck from either side. The one who came up to the shotgun side, drinking a beer, was loud and very aggressive. They both engaged in verbal harassment and one incessantly kept saying "Drink up, Stud," and trying to get Shorty to roll his window down more than the crack that he had. After their attempts fell short and it dawned on them that they would not be associated with in any manner, the one on the passenger side threw his can of beer at the window. Luckily, most of the beer was gone and the can mostly hit the frame more so than the glass.

  I knew it was getting hot, so I quickly readied the M-1 carbine that I'd been given with the banana clip and positioned myself at the port-hole which would give me a clear view and shot if warranted. Some of what was said I could make out, some, not so clear—or I was distracted in preppin' myself. I was already ready to lay them down after the throwing of the beer can. Yet, I knew to bide my time. Keep my eyes glued to their hands. If either one ever so much as acted like he was reaching for something, I was duty bound to lay him down. As it were, it was two on two. I allowed things to run its course. After the guy on the passenger side became even more frustrated because Shorty just wouldn't roll his window all the way down, the woodchuck would be right winger. He started issuing threats on what all he'd do if Shorty didn't open the door.

  We were on a road far outside of a city. We deliberately kept to the less than normal routes. I continued to shuffle from one hole to another so as to see if any vehicle was coming. Nothing! Good! When I felt we had done our best to be polite and the two chucks still would not retire, I said unto myself, "Fuckit'!" I hit the latch, popped up and pointed the carbine at the one on Comrade Shorty's side. "If ya got kids, you should've played with them." Then I squeezed. I hit the one nearest Shorty in the left of his neck, downing him immediately. I turned my attention to his potnah nearest Comrade Louis, instructed him to move to the side of the road. He complied. I then put one directly in his head and he flew backwards. I jumped out the U-Haul, walked over to the one bleeding out from his jugular and put two more in his head. Then, I moved to the other one, stood over him and blasted him two more times. I still had that "tray" concept in me. It seems to come natural wherever I go and whatever I do when a weapon is involved.

  We gave it to our best to hide the two woods. Shorty got in their jeep and drove behind us until such time as it was deemed we had come across a good spot to place the jeep. Completed, we were on our merry way again. From time to time, we'd stop and this would grant my 'rades opportunity to surface anything deemed relevant. Something such as what took place with the woodchucks in Utah. Of which, I was not scolded or accused of being over-reactive; just "informed" on how to detect whether or not such a situation was a true threat or more adventurism in the form of racial hatred and curiosity all rolled into one. I listened and I learned, while tossing the silver dollar I'd removed from the loud one's person. I flashed to my big homie, Eldridge, and what he'd sometimes say: "A lesson well taught is a lesson well learned." Indeed if one looks and listens, they will learn. Me HTTTT (Here To Tell The Truth).

I returned to the U-Haul, locked myself in, whipped out my pocket-sized dictionary Huey gave me, and commenced to study.

We went through Colorado without incident, but this was not the case in Tennessee. While traveling through the state of Tennessee, we would encounter more racists. These, a bit older, and three in number as opposed to the two back in Utah. The entire south was experiencing one of the worst floods on record, causing people out and about to have to take alternative routes. This forced us to travel across land replete with folk of truculent character in an already inimical place. Yet we did what we had to do, keeping it moving. If something popped up and needed to be redressed, that we did, and moved on. I was learning to be cognizant at every turn. Tennessee is a state where its oligarchy is vicious. I did a lot of traveling while in the army but that was very different. There were set rules and routes, and there was also the very important fact that all this was approved, so to speak. Traveling alone—especially if you are Black and in the south—anything can happen at almost any time.

While in Tennessee, we were forced to scrap our chosen route and advance through several small "hick towns" at our own risk. Aside from stopping for gas, and this didn't occur until we had used the gas we'd purchased and stashed in the back of the truck, we did not stop. We pushed the International truck to the max. It never once gave us a minute's trouble. We only experienced a problem when, rolling through some small spot not even on the map, somehow the U-Haul came loose. It rolled down a small embankment, and we knew it was going to be a major problem to get it back up on the road. At the time when it came a-loose, nobody was in it. We had stopped way deep along come country road, pouring rain, and thundering and lightning. It would occur seemingly on its own. Perhaps we had hit one bump in the road too many. Who knows? However, what we do know is, while stopped on the misadventure of the run-away U-Haul, as fate and destiny would have it, along came a spider in the form of three 'woods in a raggedy station wagon. Odds are, we were on their land. But at the moment, that was the least of our worries.

They pulled over directly in front of our truck. Instantly I moved to the back of the U-Haul, leaned against it, and watched their every move. I was wet, cold, very hungry, and yet to have, in my opinion, the full measure of recompense for what the 'woods did to me and mine back in California. They exited their station wagon and walked back towards us. As is the case whenever there are two or more people, someone always step up and take the lead role. One 'wood began to speak in a slow drag that some southerners are known for. "What y'all boys doing way out here?" he said. To which Louis replied "Just trying to get home." The second 'wood, the larger of the three, butted in and asked "Where's home?" Louis maintained the lead and replied, "Still a good ways." There were sizing us up. Engagin' in verbal gymnastics, as it were, to see if they may can take from us whatever we may have had of value, or even worse.

Their first lead spoke again. "Well, y'all know it's rough out here, spesh'lee in this here kinda weather. Y'all lost o' somp'in? Louis replied, "Naaa, we're ok, just had to make adjustments. We're going to be moving on right now. You guys have a safe one and stay warm."

From where we all stood, they could not see the back of the U-Haul—or me—clearly. They had to peep me when they first drove up, so we knew it was three of us just like we knew it was three of them. The U-Haul had went down a small embankment, perhaps three feet or so. It was not so steep that we could not get it back up and on the road. It was more so that it was very heavy. I played my hand like a natural man. I addressed Louis. "Wont some beef jerky?" I said as I positioned myself directly at the back of the U-Haul all in one motion. I didn't open it up, just left it unlocked and accessible, if necessary.

Exchanges were made, and one 'wood concerned himself with the way we talk, and we didn't sound southern enough for his liking. Shorty, as usual, didn't say much. Like always, he let Louis do the talking. Shorty was like me: a man of action. He was very short, perhaps 5'2, with Chinese eyes. He kept his hair braided into small braids with a kufi cap worn by Muslims on his head almost all the time. He would take it off 'pending where we were and what we were doing or fixing to do. In addition, we had standing symbols which, if done, we knew how to respond. We knew, for example, if any one of us pat our self on the left shoulder with the palm of the hand, endeavor to get your weapon. If anyone at any time put both hands on their hips, it was cool; no need to get alarmed. If any one of us crossed his arms at any time, we knew danger was afoot. Shorty had crossed his arms.

As I played it off like I was getting some beef jerky, the 'woods continued in their investigation. When I reappeared from the back of the U-Haul, I was in the company of my shownuff-shownuff potnah. His name was simply M-1. I aimed it at the 'wood who'd been asking all the questions and told him, "Dig, get ya ass down there and help get this trailer out this gully. Don't say shit to me, don't even look my way. If you even so much as hesitate, I'll put a hole in ya ass the size of the Grand Canyon." The 'woods hurried up and commenced to trying their best to get the trailer out. Louis and Shorty jumped in and helped out while I kept the wolves at bay. After several attempts and endeavors this way and that, they finally got it up on the road where Shorty reattached it again.

With the trailer re-stabilized, everyone could be on their merry way. I noticed Shorty again with his arms crossed. I looked at him closely to make sure I was not reading him wrong. He maintained his position. It was clear; there was no mistake. In a split second, I united the thunder, lightning, and the blast to the M-1 to the lead 'wood's. The weather turning out to be an ally, so to speak.

The remaining two panicked and mumbled something to which I paid no attention. Instead, I opened fire on the both of them. I hit one of them directly in the temple and he collapsed to the ground immediately. Then I blasted the last 'wood standing, after repeating to him to put his hands down. He yelled and screamed, "I ain't done nuthin' man!" I said back to him, "Yes you did: you were born." And with that, I blasted him in his liver. A shot Shorty himself showed me and told me of its consequences if not taken to a hospital in 11 minutes. He fell where he stood. I then walked over to the "interrogator," looked down at him and put the barrel near his throat and squeezed again. I then moved on to his potnah, looked down at him, quickly concluded to place one in his forehead, to which I did exactly that. Then I blasted him in his heart. In short, I expended nine of my own personal stash. Louis and Shorty cautioned me about wasting ammo when it was clear that the victim was surely already dead. Still, I left my seven-tray mark, nonetheless. Fuckit!

We rolled on.

We arrived in Louisiana. We made our way to a small town with no sidewalks. It was called Slidell, pronounced SLY-DELL. Once there, everyone was introduced. It was said I was the youngest brother ever recruited into the military wing of the Black Liberation Army on the entire west coast. I laid bare all I had learned from Uncle Sam. We practiced martial arts each and every morning without fail and regardless of weather. We learned how to break all weapons down blind folded and within a specific amount of time. We had established safe houses throughout the South, especially in Georgia, Alabama, Louisiana and Mississippi. We would sometimes leave on missions to ain't no telling, perhaps St. Louis where we had to castigate an individual. We also traveled up to New York and corrected an individual. Then we would return back to Louisiana.

Me personally, I knew the lay of the land fairly well. I clearly understood my location from when I was a mere child to when I was in basic training at Ft. Polk, Louisiana. I knew I was right next door to a place I longed to return to and avenge my grandfather and his comrade, Brother Medgar Evers. I was next door to Mississippi, the birthplace of my dear mother and the selfsame place that raped and killed her twin sister. I had secretly longed to return to Mississippi and, in real true life, lynch me a cracker! Dam skippy, I never put an "n" at the end of "dam" because true radicals don't believe it is necessary. Thus, I spell it "dam" on purpose. Nothing to do with bad grammar or illiteracy. It is purely deliberate. Mississippi. Yeah, I most certainly longed to play "prodigal son" in contemporary times only to return and wreak sheer havoc. Lynch me a cracker. And not just any cracker. No! I wanted it to be a sheriff! Dam right. Lynch me a sheriff right there in 'Sip! I took a self-imposed constitution to (1) never forget what they (crackers) did to my beloved grandfather. Murdered him and Brother Medgar Evers, tossing my grandfather's body in the swamps. How they murdered my mother's twin sister. They raped her. Four crackers. Then forced poison down her throat, then forced her panties down her throat, too. Then left her for the animals and insects to have a field day on. It straight gnawed at me. I promised myself I'd never forget or forgive. Let the would-be so called Christians do the forgiving shit. Me, Ashanti, I ain't forgiving nobody for shit. Me, each and every chance I get, I plan to put my foot in their ass. That's my idea of forgiving. It was considered risky business to even slightly suggest unto me to forgive woodchucks for all they had done to my race. If you said it and I heard it, or it got back to me, you'd best do like Brother KRS-1 said and "Duck down!"

My comrades constantly lectured my on prioritizing things. I was learning, but when something is branded very-very-very deep in your brain, it is truly hard. A constant battle. An eternal war. I endeavored to put my best foot forward. When we were not on missions or other raids, other comrades and I—male and female—had to read 16 hours a day. We had to discuss the content of each chapter entailed in each book. Initially, I complained and used as an excuse, "I'm from the ghetto, man. I grew up smoking weed and fuckin' with acid and dranking and shit every day. I didn't never go to no dam school." The comrades were not trying to hear it. "Study!" be the word! So study I did. We read some of everything. We were not permitted to interact with our sisters save normal activity. Activity which would inevitably lead to romantic behavior was not permitted. Today, I not only understand it, but fully support it and advertise it to all who will listen. So, reading was the word. I had learned much. I was no longer an indifferent, cold-blooded killer. Today, if it was not going to help my entire race—I reiterate as Huey used to love to say—my entire race, then it must be placed in its proper category. If or when the time surfaces for it to be exhumed, then it will be. But, not before then. Today, it about the people's struggle. Moreover, I knew if it was meant to be, one day, I'd get me a peck-ass so-called sheriff for what he did to my grandfather. And for what them pigs did to cover up what they did to my grandfather and Brother Medgar. And for what they all did, whatever part they played in covering up what them bastards did to my mother's twin sister. A deed that made my mother come unglued and she was never whole again. Never! Forgive, alright. Break my foot off in as many of 'um ass I possibly could was more like it. That was my definition of "forgiveness." Continued to live in my head, rent free. I knew I'd either soon have to evict the thought or charge it rent.

Back at the safe house in Slidell, learning remained at the top of the list, right along with safety. One beautiful day, we are up. We finish washing up—the brothers did—and we go outside. I remember it clearly as if happened just seconds ago. We were stretching and warming up to practice the arts. I was leading the comrades, aside from Shorty and Louis, who at this point I had come to learn were Al-Tanins (The Dragons). Louis was Pmoja, his true, cultural name. Shorty was Imoja, his righteous cultural name. I spoke on how I used to put my gun up the asshole of a fag and blast him. The brothers from places such as New York, and comrades there from Decatur, Georgia, were shocked. Sometimes I'd be intentionally graphic as possible to leave an indelible imprint. More than a couple of times, comrades accused me of exaggerating, and sometimes of making it up altogether. But I said to myself, they just don't know. This once was an everyday thang. Pimps and punks needed to know that pimps and punks gotta go, I said to myself. Like Victor used to say. So, we stretched and got loose. It was a very warm Louisiana day. Slidell is right across from New Orleans, just like Oakland and Frisco right across the golden. Same thing, except Slidell had dirt roads instead of streets. But people were far and away friendlier than say, Oakland. Oakland, man, you better not look at a dude twice. No telling what might jump. In Slidell, people went out of their way to speak, greet you, and ask you questions. I loved it. The fresh air. The trees. It was all good. Totally the opposite of California, where I was born.

As we stretched and warmed up, from nowhere, a lime-green truck passed by. I caught sight of it out of the corner of my eye. Then, a flash. One of the comrades spoke out, "Hey, did anyone see what I just saw?" I said, "Yeah, I saw a flash." Then Comrade Imoja said, "I saw it, too. Go and report it to the commander, JaJa." I rushed into the house, sought our commander who, for reasons need not be known, we called "Gomer Pyle." All comrades knew what it meant. I told our commander what had just occurred. He said, "Go after them. Do not harm them, though. We do not know for certain who they are or what they are doing. Just arrest the camera from them and destroy the film. Be certain you do only that." I rushed back outside and told my comrades. Imoja produced keys to the International truck. Three jumped into the cab with Imoja at the wheel. Two jumped into the back. We raced off with the intent to track down and retrieve the film from whoever it was that snapped that picture of us.

With the roads as they were, we soon caught up to the lime green truck. As we did, they did not make any effort to try to outrun us. They continued on a normal rate of speed. It was hard to pull up alongside them on the type of road we were on, but when the opportunity availed itself, we did. We asked them to pull over. The truck had two white males in it. About in their early 40s. They all of a sudden slightly sped up, turned slightly as to where their truck did a half spin. They both jumped out, drew weapons and yelled, "FBI! Get out of the truck, now! Everybody keep your hands on the truck." I heard one of the two get on his radio and request back-up ASAP. Until their arrival, we did not move. Like statues there in the hot Louisiana sun, we waited. Wasn't long before we were being entertained by pigs asking more question than the law allows. Their main question: "Where is Gomer Pyle? We know he's somewhere here in Slidell. That's why you guys are here. Where's Gomer Pyle?"

In posthaste, we rushed after these pigs, and we did so forgetting to take arms along. It actually may have been a blessing in disguise because if we had weapons on the scene, we surely would have engaged them in a shoot-out. With the firepower we had, we would have probably killed the both of them without much of a fight. How serious would that have been?

Notwithstanding, Pmoja, Imoja and I didn't know exactly what the feds knew in regards to what all had been involved during our making our way here to Louisiana. Plus, we still had the sawed-off we found in the station wagon of the three I laid down in Tennessee. We knew without even speaking, if they raided the safe house, the grenades alone will send everybody to the feds probably for life. I had Jamilah pregnant with my child going to be showing up in a sec. We all knew what they meant as well as why they wanted someone known as Gomer Pyle. Yet we imitated Sgt. Shultz: "I know nothing! Nothing!"

For unexplainable reasons, somethings stirred in me. I said aloud, "Can I talk to somebody, please? I need to talk to somebody, please. It's important." One of the feds fairly near me asked what was the matter. I told him, "Look in my wallet, sir. I just got out of the U.S. Army. I was stationed at Fort Polk. You can check it. I got a ride from these guys because I'm trying to find some family members I never met in New Orleans. I got a ride from this guy. I don't know none of these guys and I most certainly never heard of nobody named Gomer Pyle. I'm just trying to find my cousins on my father's side who stay in some place called the Third Ward or something like that. That's all I know. I don't know what's going on here and I don't want to get caught up in none of it. I'm fixing to be a father. Who do I need to speak with to settle this matter?" For whatever reason, the FBI took my wallet, noticed that I did in fact have military papers in it. He went and got on the radio in their car for a few minutes. Then he returned and said, "Mr. Jackson, next time catch a cab or call somebody. Now get out of here."

I looked at the Comrade Pmoja and Imoja with near tears in my eyes. Knowing me as they did, they knew I'd go get weapons and return regardless to what Gomer Pyle, Jesus, Muhammad, Allah, Yaweh and whoever else had something to say about it. They knew. Under his breath, Pmoja said, "Save the sisters!" That was the last time I ever seen my 'rades. I made it back to the safe house, constantly looking over my shoulder. It took a while for we had drove further from the safe house than it initially seemed. By the time I got back and ran it by sister Iyana and Gomer Pyle, a good 45 minutes or better had already gone by. I received instructions to get the sisters and the U-Haul to New Orleans. Secure the sisters and the U-Haul and wait until you're contacted. I did exactly that.

We chopped it with some people nearby, got them to accept a 20 dollar bill in exchange for making a few phone calls for me. They called my father's home and obtained information I needed, then called and called until they got my cousin Bernice on the phone. Made her aware that I was on my way. And lastly, they called a taxi for me. When the taxi showed, we talk to the brother. Got him to understand that I was new here, fresh out of Sam's Army and trying to locate my family I'd never met before who lived in the Fifth Ward in New Orleans. Her name was Bernice Nixon. I slipped him an extra 50 and he hurried-up and hooked the U-Haul onto the taxi and we were off to New Orleans. As we drove across the bridge, the taxi driver explained to us this was the "longest bridge in the world." It stretched the Mississippi River. We drove as I looked, listened and learned.

Once we reached New Orleans, it reminded me of Frisco. Lots of people on the move, plenty of hills and it smelled of sea food. It was fun. Seemed to have bowling alleys on dam-near every corner. If not, a liquor store. Bomb bow-legged sisters everywhere. The cab driver knew his way around and in no time we were in front of some long, dark brownish looking dwellings they call "The Wards." It was almost night time when we finally found my Cousin Bernice's residence. I hopped out, ran up to the door and knocked. Bernice came to the door. When she opened it, she yelled, "Michael!" I said, "What's up, Bernice?" She said, "Come on in." I stepped inside, copped a squat and began to explain to her I needed her help. I am someone in a bind. I have some beautiful sisters with me. I also have a U-

Haul trailer, and not to concern herself with the money part—we got loot so don't trip. She told me she was not married but had a boyfriend. He was a mechanic and his name was Bernard. She told me, "Go get them girls." So I broke wide, fetched the sisters, paid and seriously thanked the taxi driver, got all our things and let him skip to my lou. We all squeezed inside. Met her children. And I noticed when she fired up the Salem, it was a doobie in the ash tray. Aww shit, I thought to myself, she smoke weed. Can't fool me. I'm from that down and dirty eastside. I know shit Johnny on the spot. No doubt, she smoked weed.

Bernice told us she'd do all she could, but her place was too small for all of us to stay there. So we worked out a plan. We got a motel. We all had loot, but the major loot was held by Pmoja, and Gomer Pyle of course. This proved to be critical. Money talks indeed. The good thing, if you can call it that, was that we were in an environment that was almost completely Black. The U-Haul sat there for three days without anyone tripping whatsoever. On the fourth day, with money seriously low, Sister-comrade Iyana, who had the most rank amongst us, suggested we set out for St. Louis. We needed a place to blueprint our plans. The motel owner was sweating sis'nem religiously over small scratch. Yet he was well within his rights. We owed him. He didn't owe us. But, we also knew well to prioritize our loot. Stretch was the operative word. We concluded with the sisters going to St. Louis. I would return to California and lay low until I was contacted. So be it.

My father contacted me and wired me some money to catch a plane out of New Orleans. I leaned with my back against the New Orleans Superdome, smoking a Salem, and thinking about what I'm gonna do when I return to California. The stories to tell Vic'nem. The Western Union where money could be wired was directly across the street from the Superdome, right on the corner. Eventually, I got the loot. Got my hugs, said my thanks, said my good-byes, and burnt rubber back to Cali.

I landed in Frisco International. Pops was there to pick me up. He asked me all sorts of questions. He knew—let Pops tell it—them boys were dangerous. I divulged what I felt was not in manifest error of our credo, and left it at that. I was alive and well and Pops settled for that. I was back in Cali. Only this time, I was truly a changed man. I had matters to redress. People had some explaining to do. What I didn't know and never tripped was that my "homeboys" were looking at me different, and were of the opinion that it was me who had some explaining to do. Runnin' off with them funny talking niggas, some of the homies said. But I musta hurried up, checked them, and got it right. I fell back in with the same old crowd. Start doing the same old thang. Messing with a gang of dope, a gang of girls and doing a gang of foul-ass, stupid, totally uncalled for shit. All to show the homies I was still down.

    I remained that way until one morning, I was about to go kick it with my home girl Veronica, when I got word those pigs in Slidell killed all the comrades. Imoja and Pmoja were DEAD! I was like, "Naw!" But the messenger was like, "Yeah." I said naw again. He said yeah, again. I looked away to gain all the strength I could to keep from straight crying. It hit me like, man I don't know what. Pmoja, Imoja. Naw. Dude must got his info crossed. Can't be. We had plans out of this world. They were far, far more to me than mere mentors, or even just comrades. They had become part of me. In just a matter of minutes, it all hit me. In just the short amount of time I'd been back in California, I had let the streets re-enter and regain control of my life. I went back inside, undressed, laid down with my fingers interlaced behind my head. I thought, real reeeeeeeeal deep, "Are you 'really' serious about being a revolutionary, JaJa? I mean reeeeeally serious?" Was it that I was merely mad at some white people because of what had happened to some of my immediate family members? Was it that I was mad about injustices that had occurred and seemingly continue to occur here in North ameriKKKa? Was it that I just didn't like white people or authorities? What was it? I needed to sort these things and questions out, conclude them once and for all and go from there. My entertaining these thoughts alone let me know that I was already heading in the right direction. From that point on, I was cool with "trippin'" with so-called homeboys. They were going nowhere doing what they were doing. I loved my people. I was deadly serious about people harming my race, and wasn't nowhere near fixing to turn my back on my sisters. That was out. I had taken an oath and meant it from the bottom of my heart. I overstood it in its entirety. I wasn't bullshitting. People had done my people wrong...for centuries. Hell naw. Vic'nem could have the streets. They could have the tray. Imoja had warned me just as Jamilah did: "I know that's your homeboy, JaJa," said Imoja one time sitting on our balcony while staying in the Huey Newton hi-rise. "But," he continued, "He's not on your level. You may not want to hear this, brother, but I can see a snake in him. You need to know and realize this." I didn't listen. I also never imagined that Vic would hold it against me for leaving California and him having to fend for self. Yet, such was the case. There were signs when we had the 'wood in my apartment and Vic never raised a hand towards the 'wood, nor did he even say a word to dude for hitting his grand homeboy (me). And nothing about how they could've killed my girl and unborn child. None of that. Those were clear signs but I missed them back then. I always felt folks was jealous of me and Vic because we had all the finest girls, kept weed, money and drank, and we were known throughout Oakland for getting in whoever's ass. There were some other signs that I should've peeped about Vic. But not matter what, the person hadn't been born yet who could convince me that it would be Vic who'd get up on the witness stand and testify on me. And would do everything in his power to have me not only charged, not only convicted of three murders, but also found guilty of special circumstance leading to the introduction of the death penalty!

It has been said that eventually, the clock on the wall will say that's all. I had also been told "be still." Just be still. If you would be still, your third eye (mind) will point the way. If you listen, you shall hear it speak. And, if you look and listen, you shall surely learn.

It was time for me to be still.

* It would be reported by the news that Ashanti's comrades were killed in a shootout with the FBI. Allegedly, one of them (Pmoja?) went for a weapon and the lethal shootings ensued. Three comrades were lost. Ironic, Ashanti's "seven-tray" was maintained, even at such a high price.

Chapter 8
The Devil Tip-Toed Into Heaven While God Slept

"You can fool some of the people some of the time,
But you can't fool all the people all the time"

(Hon. Elijah Muhammad)

Upon my return, things would never be like times past. It was like Victor and I spoke two different languages. Oftentimes, I would deliberately shake Victor to the left. Aside from chasing after females and getting high, there wasn't really anything left. All else was totally cosmetic. Inside Victor, a true definition of the term "cock hound" was alive and well. Victor was not reputed as being a bona fide hustler. He got by with little. He engaged in even less still from day to day. His life was all about whatever came his way. Money, dope, sex. All else seemed to not even matter to Victor. He had no wheels, no source of income, still lived with his parents and two sisters, Donna and Linda. He engaged opportunities, indeed life itself, based on his handsome looks and ability to "woo" females seemingly at will. In the breast of Ashanti dwelled a burning. Ashanti wanted to be involved in a great many things. Even more so now that his two major comrades were resting in peace. All the more so still, being that they were killed by whitefolk. Pigs! Inside Ashanti dwelled the capacity to learn; to show what he knew; to question philosophies of sort; to read and to call into question various books and politics. And he was certainly a student of history. In addition to all this, Ashanti was a reputed drummer and could also play key-boards, and once won best drummer in the entire Bay Area back in the mid-sixties. This would cause other musicians to take a second look at me. People I grew up around, such as Sly Stone, Larry Graham, the Sledges (especially my big home girl Rita Sledge) who allowed me to play drums for their group. Abbreviated as it was, nonetheless the experience was there. World-famous Sheila E, who was just a baby when I was on the scene, but her family stayed at the end of the block in the same neighborhood. And there were plenty of others, too. Richard "Dimples" Fields, a very close friend of my brother, CJ. We once car-pooled together to and from General Motors and also went to the same church, New Hope Baptist on the north side of Oakland. There were many for me to draw from. These are just a few in the music world. In the sports and entertainment world there existed far more people. Every opportunity seemed to avail itself at the feet of Ashanti. The $64,000 Question was what, if anything, would Ashanti do with them?

Stirring deep within me were the images I'd seed from Comrades Pmoja and Imoja when we all lived on the same floor in the Huey Newton Hi-rise. Ashanti remembered well what he had learned from both Black Buddha and the likes of Donald "Cinque" DeFreeze, who also stayed on the very same floor with Comrade Pmoja, Imoja and me. And let us not forget the Puerto Rican, Juan. As crazy as it may sound, me and good old Juan's encounters were not quite finished. We would run into each other. A head-on collision inside the infamous San Quentin. As fate and Destiny would have it, Juan—for reason only he and his Creator will ever know—hung himself in San Quentin. Juan would be found hanging from a vent with torn sheets made into a rope around his neck, dead.

Truth be told, Juan's death did not really disturb me. If I didn't know anything else, I was well-versed in people I knew "meeting their maker" for one reason or another. But few, if any, died of natural causes, perhaps save the one individual killed by lightning directly in front of me when I was a child. Yet and still, even that I carried with me wherever I went.

Back in Oakland from New Orleans, however, I had to find myself. Discover just what I intended to do with the remainder of my life. It was really not that hard a choice. Either continue to play music and go on to play at a professional level, or engage in the people's struggles full-time. I elected the latter, and did so remarkably fast. The situation of my people was far and away more important than playing music. Well did I keep it uppermost in my mind the Emmitt Tills of times past. And of contemporary times. I had met Brother-comrade Alprentice "Bunchy" Carter and many other freedom fighters at the Oakland Auditorium when the largest group of revolutionaries met there. The varying guest speakers seriously turned it out. From a young age, both me and brothers I ran with, such as Victor Jackson (no relation), and Ronnie Brown, who would grow up to be recognized around the world for his prowess in martial arts. Ronnie joined a martial arts studio around 1969 or so. Ronnie and I were tight as tight could get coming up a kids. Not in my wildest dreams did I or could I **ever** imagine that Ronnie would join ranks with Victor to get me off the streets. There was also Harold Warrick, who also joined the martial arts studio with his childhood friend Ronnie. Often Ronnie and Harold would try to convince me and Victor to come to the martial arts studio, but to no avail. My reply to the both of them was simple: "I use guns, blood!" Once in a while, Harold would tag along me, Victor and Ronnie when we would go "on a mission" and snatch up some jezebel and set her vagina on fire. But normally, it would just be Vic and me.

There would be occasion when words were exchanged and things got heated between myself and Harold Warrick. One such incident occurred when I spotted all the homies to go see Brother Curtis Mayfield, Tower of

Power and the Barkays at Winterland. I paid for the tickets, the weed, the al-key—everything. Yet Harold had two words to say about my organizing the event. I told him, "Check this out, blood. If you don't like how we gon' get down, stay ya ass at home." He said something to the effect of (kinda under his breath because he knew I was strapped and that I dam sure knew how to use it quick…hella quick at that), "Like you runnin' shit." I stopped dead in my tracks as I was about to unlock the car door on their side. I turned to confront his lil' Bruce Lee wanna-be-ass, and said, "Dig, blood. If I ever hear you say anything else about what I do or how I do it, or I hear anything about you trippin' or feeling sympathetic for them 'woods, I'll put my gun in yo' mouth and squeeze 'til I run outta bullets."

We all knew each other, grew up together from elementary all the way through high school. Harold, good as he was becoming with the arts, didn't want to see me about nothing. He knew I was an expert on catching people slippin'. I had no more problems out of Mr. Warrick. Yet I knew all along he didn't really care for me, especially after that. He was funny-style anyway. Fuck-em' and feed-em' fish was my position.

I revisited some of the old spots. The Lamp Post, the old favorite hangout of the panthers of yesteryear. It wasn't nowhere near like it was in its heyday when Huey and Eldridge'nem used to slide through. I used my father's old "work-car" to blend and went back to the West Side to see what I could see. I hit up the California Hotel area, all up and down San Pablo. Prostitutes galore. It was like we had never existed. Like we never put in work. Perhaps the so-called pimps now had relaxed and maybe, just maybe, weren't even concerned about the once-upon-a-time contract on me. I saw pimps galore all up and down the Aves'. I drove by the Tiki Club on San Pablo, said to be owned by the notorious Ward Brothers. One of them, Frank Ward, supposedly the oldest of the bunch, pulled a .38 on me and my boy, Montgomery. This because we had it that we were the ones snatching up—as he called it—his hoes. This took place on the West Side where the so-called pimps, punks and prostitutes are super thick. A while back, Ronnie Brown and I snatched a slut up off the stroll. It had been a while, but proper tactics versus greed/ money, proper tactics will win out each and every time. We pulled her, isolated ourselves, removed her from the car, whooped that ass, knocking her unconscious. That accomplished, we positioned her in such a way as to where nothing was touching the earth but her shoulder blades. I baptized her "monkey" in the name of the people's struggle, in the name of all the people you and your peers done gave STDs, and in the name of right versus wrong. Her monkey was now so replete with gas it spilt over. I told Ronnie, "Let the shit run all down to her asshole." This would hopefully serve notice that we were back and that such activity would not be tolerated. Montgomery, somewhat new in the hood from the south, started hanging with us. We used to tell him of our deeds and objectives. ALWAYS WHITE GIRLS. We never "torched" a sister. Never! Montgomery didn't believe us. I told him, "One time, we're gonna take you on a mission with us." The aforementioned regarding Frank Ward pulling a .38 on me, was that time. When we approached a hooker, she played her hand and apparently they had devised some signal and the so-called pimp knew we were trying to pull one of his. They rushed in to save her and to deal with us, their arch nemesis.

What saved us was we were right down the street from Del Monte cannery, and some females were right on the corner, waiting on the bus. I yelled to the sisters in the most serious voice I could, "Aye. Aye, Sister. Dig, these dudes are trying to make us get in their car. They gonna take us on a gangsta ride. You know what that mean? Y'all know what gangsta ride mean?" The sisters, coincidentally three in number, advanced towards us, saying, "What y'all doing wit dem young boys? Y'all better leev'dem 'lone ah we ah call da police!" I kept yelling, for I knew that the two brothers who had drove up in the "doo-doo brown" Electra 225 were hit men for Frank Ward. He and his two henchmen-three. I yelled to the sisters, "Get their license number, sisters! Write it down! Don't try to remember it, write it down!" Frank Ward tucked the .38 in his jet-black turtleneck, slowly backed away saying, "Yeah! We know what you look like! Yeah, we know who you is now mu'fucka! Y'all dead!" He climbed back into his snow-white coup, started it, gunned it, and disappeared. The two brothers in the Electra followed suit, never saying a word. Montgomery and I cut the hell out as fast as we could. I learned from that. It was over. Gotta be a better way to teach the people. Besides, I later thought, setting white bitches' pussies on fire, shiiiit, I'm no better than the ones that killed my mother's twin sister. I concerned a great amount of time on whether it was justifiable to "torch a white bitch." Hell, I didn't even call NO sister "bitch." That was reserved solely for snow bunnies (white girls). I sent the mental jury out. Such came back with a verdict: not guilty. So, consequently, I never "torched another Jezebel." I decided to find another way to endeavor to correct the wrongs that had been and continued to be inflicted on my people. The words of my C-homie, Eldridge Clever haunted me.

I am not at liberty to speak about what and how I came to prison. Suffice it to say, I was convicted of three first degree murders of well-to-do whites. Said to have been Morons. I wouldn't know. There came a time that the FBI took me in and questioned me with regard to some bomb threats issued and a communique, and they also spoke at length about my involvement in some expropriated armored truck money. They made me write the entire front page of a newspaper on a writing pad they provided. When I finished writing the entire front page, one of them said, "Now print it!" After I engaged in all they served me with, they let me go. Not enough evidence.

I constantly held conferences with self. I also, again, established a large cleavage between my so-called homeboys, larger than the one when I was with my newfound comrades. This time, however, I didn't care if they endorsed it or not. Being I had undergone a serious change, the people I elected to associate myself with also underwent a radical change. Such stands to reason.

I chanced upon an old homie, Ray Doyle Gray, who was straight from the hood. Actually, I should've known better because, once, Ray Doyle as we called him, erroneously accused my brother and I of burning his garage down. I ran across Ray Doyle on the streets of east Oakland. At that time, Ray Doyle had escaped from the California Department of Corrections (CDC). He was on the run. He needed, among other things, a safe place to stay. We kicked it for a minute then departed. What I will say about Ray Doyle Gray is this: he was paid money by OPD (Oakland Police Department) to lie and testify against me. Ray Doyle taking the witness stand against me, along with Victor Jackson, Ronnie Brown, and Harold Warrick got me convicted of three murders. They also introduced the so-called special circumstance phase, which I was found guilty of. Enter the death penalty. My so-called "homies!" Here I sit, just about 40 years flat on the nose. Not quite 40 yet. I'm right there now, knocking on the door of a 40-ounce. Said it before, will say it yet again: my would-be so-called homeboys. I'd hope that all who chance upon these words recognize that 1) Ashanti is not proud of what he did. 2) I don't think I'm hard, and this, I am not. Just because one engages in irrational behavior does not constitute him, her, or them as being hard, raw, or the shit as we sometimes say. Well, wake-up call, that's not true. Today, it's totally about out-thinking your opposition. Trust me, dear reader, when I tell you I know this to be true first hand.

At the end of the day, I would hope that this book would serve to encompass for all those heading in the wrong direction. I am not here to preach, for I am not a minister. However, I am well learned in various other fields. Being misguided, especially by those you trust, respect, and had complete confidence in—such is my lot. As a youth, one often hears elders say, "If I could do it all over again!" Today, as opposed to this "prison," I wish I could have stuck to playing music. It was a natural gift and it came easy. I could read, write, and play music when I was in the 5th grade. Talent, wasted. On the flip side of the coin, I will not be found being apologetic for what all I became involved in and/ nor for the methods employed in effort to get a point across. Vicious as they were. All this makes up the sum total of who I am today. Without going through what I did, I would not be able to speak from a position of surety. This, I know!

It was my intent to help Ray Doyle. I gave him a little money, some weed, and some cigarettes. What I didn't know was Ray Doyle was still shooting up "dog food."[15] As much as he could get. "China White!" We talked about doing some things, but he was never my cup of tea. Plus, we seldom, if ever, saw one another. We were never tight like Vic, Ronnie, Dex, and me. It would me my homie Dexter English's sister, sweet Donna whom I dated for the longest, who cautioned me about socializing with Ray Doyle. A brother who also grew up in the hood, Ray Doyle and Dexter stayed much closer than Ray Doyle and I.

Again, because I am still waging combat with regard to my case, I cannot delve deep into it. Suffice it to say, it was Ray Doyle Gray's testimony that hurt me the worst. Victor, Ronnie, and Harold's testimonies were what are known as "character" witnesses. They got on the stand and spoke to the jury about things they seen me do. Totally 100% inimical deeds. They gave details of me pouring both lighter fluid and gas in the ear of many fags and lighting it, etc. This, along with Ray Doyle's words, was what did it. I was finished. Best friends turned worst enemies. I was painted upon the jury to look like the older brother in Clockwork Orange!

---

[15] Heroin. *http://urbandictionary.com.*

Next thing I know I heard the words, "Next stop, SAN QUENTIN!" Or as we convicts called it, Dracula's Castle, because of the way it looked.

I absolutely hated San Quentin. Actually, there was nothing to like about it. The weather was horribly cold year round because of its location. You were surrounded by water. The Pacific Ocean with a divide they call The Bay. San Quentin, especially when I was there, was a prison for older convicts. It was five tiers high. People were out of their cells rippin' and runnin' all day and night until lock-up time at 9 p.m. There were some arsons on a regular basis. They sold Ronson's Lighter Fluid in the exact same blue and yellow can that I had so frequently used on the streets when I was out doing dirt. How ironic, I thought. Music blared. Almost all the windows were broken out—this was mostly done by the whites, drunk and indifferent. Even worse still, come the end of the year, the prisoners were absolutely notorious for "flooding" tiers and burning blankets. These gave off fumes that burnt your lungs something terrible and it was accompanied by a thick, black smoke. They would carry on late into the night, with no respite.

I quickly learned that Quentin was also just replete with drugs. Whatever they had on the streets, you could rest assured it was on the tiers of San Quentin. Just like whatever they had for dinner that day, it was guaranteed to be on the tier for sale that selfsame night. Fags (so-called homosexuals) pranced to and fro. Gangs were very evident at every turn. Black, white, Mexican—all had staked out turf. Brothers would pull youngsters to the side and school them (sit them on their lap, as it was called). 'Pending who you were, or if you had or have family in the pen, you may be invited to move hither and yon. There were any number of characters imaginable. Some were into the Bible and some were into the Quran. Jews were present too but, very low-key. Aryans were very visible, and perhaps, the most lethal. They had something no other convicts had: the man. Police and whites worked hand in hand in San Quentin, certainly anything but a big Masonic secret. Later, while at DVI (Deuel Vocational Institution) in Tracy, where I was charged with murder, there were guns found there. Once, in the gym, a tre-five-seven (.357 Magnum) and a Derringer were found in the bleachers. Police were actually, and in real true life, "sent home" because they had the gall to wear their Klan outfits to work. Imagine that! Guards at a prison wearing their KKK get-ups to work at the prison itself. Well, they did. There were also straight Bowie knives, butcher knives, and from time to time, various forms of poison, including rat poison, razor blades and/ or broken glass discovered in our food. Both mice and rats were ever-present, along with bats galore. Stray cats, and at Folsom, a red-tailed hawk and pigeons flew freely inside the buildings themselves, with no concern by staff to get rid of them. Mice would often eat their way into a package received from fam or friends. San Quentin was really rough. Sex was so rampant in the visiting room that it started a war—the Muslims jammed the bikers about doing the do-all in front of whoever with indifference!

Sisters in the forefront, became directly involved. My then wife, Jamilah, was right in the thick of things. They (females) not only got down in the room itself with the white females when the brothers and the whiteboys gottum up, but sisters didn't stop there. They took it outside and commenced to "rat-pack" snow bunnies in route back to their cars and such, so much so that the news media began having a field day with it. The warden gave a decree: "If the convicts don't hurry up and work it out, we then will begin having Blacks visiting on Mondays, Wednesdays, Fridays; whites will have visits on Tuesdays, Thursdays, Saturdays. There will be no visiting for anybody at San Quentin on Sundays." It was worked out....for a time.

Killings were the norm at San Quentin. It quickly became normal for me to hear some Mexican bashed another Mexican in the head with a pipe. White boys attacked and killed a 'wood in the barbershop area. Used the scissors to rip his abdomen open and, with their bare hands, stuck them inside dude and pulled out his organs. A means to be more than sure "he was indeed dead." Brothers did their fair share of dirt and Black on Black shit, too...name, it, I seen it. From dude being stabbed and tossed off the tier to a dude being stabbed with a long yellow pencil through the eye and killed right there, Johnny-on-the-spot. Seen Indians doing their thang, too. There was no exception because there were no rules. It was the old Isaac Hayes verbiage: "DO YO THANG!!!" Survival of the fittest, indeed.

While I was in Oakland Courthouse Jail or OCJ, I met some of everybody. Even my boy, Eldridge, would pop up. We were cellies there. My father knew things and people I myself didn't know he was up on. He used to talk to this brother knowns as Hasimu there in CHJ. I was there for two years and seven months fighting three murders. My father also used to chop it up with a brother—perhaps the most vicious I ever met in my life—named Muhammad. His slave name was Cornell Nolan, big brother of W.L. Nolan. Straight from Oakland and as vicious as they come. Nell, as we called him, hated bullies more than anything else. Nell stood 6'4" and weighed about 230 pounds. He had fought the likes of Archie Moore, Sonny Liston, and his last fight, he fought Ken Norton. Cornell was our everything. He taught us to fast, how to make "penicillin" out of regular old everyday bread, and how to deal with a knife attack (if you see it coming). He would harp on schooling brother Azikiwe Kambon (x-Marion Craig, Fleeta Drumgo's brother), and myself on how to wage combat, of sort. Don't hesitate, just go off, he'd say. He and Brother Hasimu Ali were very tight with my father. Cornell/ Muhammad, well he was with the Nation of Islam (NOI), and Hasimu was with the Black Guerilla Family (BGF). Hasimu was at the time a chairman and was back in the CHJ only to testify on behalf of another family member. I would be his celly while there. It would be Hasimu Ali, x-Steven Browning, who would give me the oath of the BGF at the request of my father and after he himself had innumerable talks with me in the wee-hours, feeling me out. Of course he knew I was slammed for triple murders. It was all on the news, and later still, all on the TV show 60 Minute with Mike Wallace. My name was all in county jail and beyond long before I got there. In addition to all this, I was a Jackson. Hasimu, like many others of the BGF, would ask my father all sorts of questions, especially in particular, about George. Everybody with a pair of nuts loved my first cousin, George Lester Jackson. It was no secret, and as soon as I hit San Quentin, the BGH was at me, non-stop. By this time though, they had split. Me, I rode and stuck with Hasimu come hell or high water. He sponsored me in and I was gonna be with his faction unto the bitter end. However, I will openly admit, I ran across a-many from the "New Man" faction, and became ultra-tight with some. Some I've even rode with in various prisons. Some, I refer to as "comrade" to this very day.

So, I annex self with the BGF, commence to put in work right there in the county jail. Mop ringer beatings, setting a guy on fire, and otherwise just jumping on dudes became the norm. I quickly established a small crew numerically and people, after a while, began calling us "The Magnificent Seven" because we were seven in number. All of us were there fighting murders, and all but three would hit San Quentin's death row, only to be booteed off not too long after arriving. California's Supreme Court would rule the death penalty constituted cruel and unusual punishment. Thus, all of us escaped with our lives. It would be my case that was the liberating factor and it is till this day in the "law books!" Hello, fellas!!!

Convicted of three first-degree murders, and now at San Quentin sporting peach fuzz, I rolled with only the best of the best. I met Rudy da Brut, who himself was down with the martial arts and once worked out with Comrade George and others. I would meet up once again with Abdul' Ahad Shahid (x-Freddie Payne), a super-vicious brother from the old guard who helped me in many, many ways. I got the opportunity to kick it with the big homie, Sterling McDowell and all three of the McCray brothers who were at San Quentin with me at the same time. Oops, my bad, there were FOUR of the McCrays there: the oldest, Curtis, now resting; Eddie Ray, also resting (beat in the head with pipes by Hell's Angels bikers); Donell and Mike who were both still alive, I'm told, and we still love each other. Donell would parole from Folsom while my celly back in '83, '84.

It would be impossible to recall all the brothers I chanced upon. Many would not make it out alive. Some returned time and again on the violation-tip. Of those, I showed no sympathy. As far as I was concerned, they somehow didn't learn the lessons from the enemy camp. Thus, they couldn't offer me any form of advice. To many, the BGF was looked upon in awe. While it remains true to this very day, they are far and away the most intelligent and savvy out of all the Black entities within the CDC (California Dept. of Corrections). The Crips, deep as they are numerically, have never had a bona fide leader. The closest would be a brother named Raymond Washington, who I met in Tracy right before he went home, only to be killed (murdered) by his own people. Other brothers shot him with a shot gun. Bloods, too, have yet to have a leader to lead them wisely to the Promised Land, so to speak.

My initial experience with Quentin was utter disgust. I knew I wasn't gonna be able to hang after my first day on the co-called mainline. There were, of course, some good brothers. However, they were few and far between. I normally hung with my boy Ripsaw who was from the same spot as me on the streets. He'd be in the 'O for a hot sec and knew folks, plus we were on the same team (BGF). We walked and talked. The first murder I ever witnessed jump off on the other side of the fence on the upper yard was when 'woods took off on a Brother Puncho, slave name Garland Berry, also a BGF member. It would be explained to me why this took place, but, it was still completely unacceptable. He was "family" and as far as I was concerned, they had killed a family member. End of discussion. Add to that, brothers were "briefing" me on the goings on in the 'O and I sponged it all up. I had major issues hearing a male refer to another male as "baby," "cute," and "fine" and all this. So, it would come to pass that my major boy, Baba (x-Robert Duncan, r.i.p.), and I decided to do something about it.

I also had a major issue with some, not all, but "some" members of the BGF, running up in my face telling me, "Comrade George had a punk, man. That's him right there. His name is Dakota or Chacota, or something like that." I told the brother who brought this weak shit to me, "It's evident you don't know what the fuck you talking 'bout because you don't even know the punk's name, mother fucker. And, as far as I'm concerned, you're not just in manifest error, but in violation of disrespecting my family, and I want a fade." He wouldn't get down with me and, afterwards, I told Comrade Ripshaw, "Ay, Rip. Dude, gotta go, Family or not." Ripsaw begged and pleaded with me to let it go, but I couldn't.

I had learned many tactics and reviewed the Art of War, and all the major spills on military philosophy. I laid in the cut and caught dude vulnerable. As been said, "Vulnerability is an exploitable weakness." I exploited his ass with three padlocks in a sock. Fucked him up real good. After much a'do, Family decided to side with me and not discipline me as Comrade George's name was on the line. He led men, not engaged in sexual activity with punks. I explained my position on the matter well, and it went away. As for the punk, he had the gall to approach me on the upper yard. He had absolutely no facial hair. And, the way he moved about, I could tell dude was hella feminine. I played his ass like a piano. I got my boy Baba to tell him I was gonna let him let him braid my hair and to sneak in Baba's cell and wait for me. After that, I owe you. The punk went for it. When he made his move during the very first unlock the next morning, Baba and I were waiting on his ass. Sho'nuff, he pranced hi lil narrow ass in the cell bigger than shit. We waited until the pig closed the back bar and went to work. The plan was to knock him out, stab him on the right side of the body, as the left side was sho'nuff-sho'nuff vital organs. Then, boot him the fuck out, letting him live so that other punks might know. Talking 'bout started a gang of shit.

Some BGF dudes, and let me be clear, when I say BGF, I do not me all—only perhaps four or five—had the nerve to try to stand up and speak on behalf of a fuckin' fag. I just be damed. I went off immediately: "Yard meeting! Yard meeting!" I yelled. When the brothers had gathered, I told them, "Man, look here. Mutherfuckers running 'round here talking about George had a punk, and that they themselves are "lifers" and it is their only salvation and all this bullshit. Dig, I wouldn't give a fuck who don't like it. Dude right there." I pointed out the brother who had said so-called positive things about brothers in the pen, being Family, it's alright to have a punk, and so on and so forth. I sorta singled him out. Made him a scapegoat. I said, "Let me tell all y'all something: I'mma Jackson. Slave name, anyway. But dig this here, none of my family fuck wit punks and I'm lighting his ass up Johnny-on-the-spot. And fuck who don't like it. Ain't none of y'all gone be allowed to run around here talking about the Jacksons fuck wit punks. That's why I knocked a patch outta blood's head. He wasn't no 'rade. Perhaps nominally, and nominally only. But, at heart, naw. We at war with this government for shit like that (allowing dudes to tongue kiss other dudes like that shit they be doing in 'Frisco and shit). Like it's hella cool. Fuck that, and fuck any and all of y'all who disagree. We revolutionaries. Freedom fighters don't fight for the right to get their knees dirty or bend over and let another male do whatever. Y'all know that I mean. And also, I hope you all took notice that I didn't call no punk or fake-ass, would-be, so-called 'rade a 'man.' My ass. That is not the ear mark of a man. There are certain things a man just won't do. Whoever got to straight out kill me before I let nan one of y'all do some punk-skit to me, take me out, muthafucka. Take me the fuck out. To allow that shit is to cheat sisters and females out of their innate rights. I called this meeting to let y'all know, if *I* catch nan one of y'all trippin' with a punk, or even so much as taking up with a punk, I'm straight smashing ya ass, win, lose, or draw!"

    A brother 'rade cut in. "Ah, brother, you be threatening brothers and whatnot. Didn't you just come off the row? Then who is you to tell us how to conduct our affairs. You ain't been here long enough to know the real about the mainline. I been on this line..." I cut in, "Dig, faggit, I ain't trying to kick it with you. Far as I'm concerned, you'zah punk. You fuckin' wit punks, that's punk shit. You'zah punk." He tried to perp like he was about to go off and all this, buffin' and puffin', but despite me being young and not long on the line, I was known for having heart, if nothing else. Dude could get his head brought to him like anybody else. I wasn't trying to hear it. "Fuck you, and fuck them punks, blood. All you bitch-ass muthafuckas can line up single file and march ya stupid good-faking-the-funk ass to the Golden Gate and do a jack-knife off the motherfucker far as I'm concerned."

Another brother stepped up to the plate. He rode with me. "You brothers know the youngster's correct. We're supposed to be leading the people towards a means that will engender armed struggle. Not armed with lip stick." Everybody busted out laughing. The brother was no joke. Extremely well respected, big Doc from that point took a liking to me. His slave name was the same as mine; Michael. Michael Murdock. Large in excess, Doc could so much as look at whoever with that glance and folks knew to break wide. From that point on, we were dam near inseparable. Later still, I gave him the name Hashima. Whenever we were in the visiting room together, and my mother (r.i.p.) was out there, they'd kick it.

Doc and I began to study together and it would be him and another comrade that would seriously lace me about the goings on in the Q. The other 'rade, Mata Musa (x-Moses Johnson), a true to form brother if ever. Mata was out of Stockton. A terribly good brother at heart. Shared everything. Extremely articulate, even more practical, and a strong debater. We never once argued. Debate was the word. Argue, hell naw. We were about learning, not remaining stagnate. So, we kept our heads in books for as long as we were in one another's company. I drew from brother Comrade, Ripsaw, Doc/ Hashima, Mata Musa and, of course, the super wise old owl, Faraji. We called him Thin Man. I was in an emotional tug of war with the BGF and the Muslims just as when I was on the streets. Only, on the streets, it was the Panthers. In here it was the BGF. On the streets, it was the Nation of Islam. In here, since the passing of the Most Honorable Elijah Muhammad in 1975, it was now the World Community of al-Islam in the West. However, there was still an entity alive and well right there in San Quentin that was out to keep the name and teaching of the Most Honorable Elijah Muhammad alive. And they didn't see eye to eye with those who broke off and commenced to follow W.D. Muhammad and Muhammad Ali right there in Quentin, not until in the distant future.

But that was yet to occur. At that time, fresh on the line in the Q, I still had my agenda. Among other things, eradicating dudes calling dudes "baby," "fine," "cute," and so forth. I just couldn't stand it. And I had a life too. I wasn't yea'bout to go nowhere. But I'd just be good and shitted on if I EVER be found running round lustin' over another dude (notice I didn't say man). As a result of my political concerns, the BGF gave a decree: "No more Black homosexuals on the line throughout the entire CDC. Either check that ass, or get dealt with." Bottom line. This was 1977. In time, I felt, some could be salvaged from their current plight, which was them suffering from a major identity crisis. Fags popped up here and there, but sho' not like they were when I first hit the line in the Q. Plenty, and I do mean many, hur'up and got some act-right.

Today, it is perhaps worse than ever. I can say this because now you have Mexicans, especially northern Mexicans who primarily run with brothers, and thus gradually began to emulate them in verbiage. The Mexicans from down south L.A., they have far more respect and are not heard using such racial epitaphs as the n-word and so forth. However, the young whiteboys, many if not most with the swastika and lightning bolts on them, are heard using and calling each other "nigga!" Yes, whiteboys here in California call each other nigga and more, just like they have a license to do so. And it is completely tolerated by the brothers. Correction, tolerated by some brothers. It will never be tolerated by all brothers. So, today, we have Black and white niggas, whites calling Mexicans nigga, and Mexicans calling both Mexicans and whiteboys nigga. I take issue with this. Yet, like my 'rade Rashid said, "With all's that's going on, pick ya war!" Unto the true-to-form revolutionary, I say, "Brothers, we got work to do."

It might be worth mentioning that when the pigs stopped brothers from wearing their red and blue bandanas back in '83, they actually did the Crips and Bloods a major favor. Almost instantly it caused people to attempt to discern who's who before they just up and take off on somebody. I've had the marking of the BGF tatted on me since '74. I regret I ever got it tattooed on me. Not that I resent I became a member. No, certainly not that. The BGF has produced some of the most slept-on revolutionaries and bona fide thinkers of the 20th century. Reader, to adduce this as fact, go do your homework!! No. I regret having this tatted on me because I didn't ever dream that it would come to this. By "this," I mean so-called "indeterminate SHU (Security Housing Units) programs." The so-called debriefing-ism! The IGI's (Institutional Gang Investigator) birth and so forth. And they really hate the BGF with a mad, mad, mad passion because of the misadventure of August 21, 1971 at San Quentin. Might I add, the pigs hate the mighty Crips far, far worse than they do the Bloods. A matter of record. Bloods in the CDC can get away with shit the Crips would dam-sho not be allowed to. Pigs will beat a Crip down in a minute. Bloods, they may be given a lil' action, but not in every instance. But as a rule of thumb, pigs outright hate Crips. No two ways about it. Anybody ever been in prison in California knows this to be true. For one, Crips are more rowdy than Bloods. They (Crips) are very outgoing, and hella loud. Bloods lay back and just mean-mugg anybody not a Blood. They are also far and away more stand-offish. On the flip side, Bloods appear to be way more political than Crips. Crips are straight street. Bloods are, if nothing else, survivors. One thing Crips and Bloods do have in common: both seem to dig messin' with them dam punks! I used to just plain roast J. Edgar Hoover all the dam time, everywhere—dining hall, in the gym, on the yard—it really didn't matter. Fag! Here it is he did all that shit he did, this punk Hoover, and come to find out, behind closed doors, dud was a straight punk. Gayer than Christmas. Ah Sagoony! Had the nerve to trip on Martin Luther King and his broad he had on the side, yet Hoover himself would run his lil' chubby ass behind closed doors and get his so-called crossdressing on like ah motherfucker. In some instances, reported by those close to him, his so-called right hand man said, "Hoover at times was not ashamed and wore dresses and other female attire with delight." Me, I believe it. I bet its hella fags in the FBI. Manchild (Jonathan Jackson) once wrote, "Pigs are punks!" I agree wholeheartedly. If there were about their slogan, "To protect and serve the community," then why are they letting punks, sluts and known hos to run hither and yon knowing they have AIDS, HIV, and STDs. Because pigs will run them all in Johnny-on-the-spot and force them to submit to a blood test and document such findings. When one pop up with AIDS, etc., why don't they lock that ass up forever and day like they did brothers I know for shit that's not even violent? Yet, Mr. Nab-ass-Jones locked up brothers at beyond an alarming rate for crumbs. Twenty-five years. Come on, man. Knock it off! Man, folks don't' get it. Me, I do. I get it sho'nuff because I have 25 years flat inside. In fact, I have 35 years flat in—and some change. Straight out. So, I know what they are facing. I advise all truly concerned to resort to and employ drastic measures to avoid being my dam celly 'cause, truth be told, I ain't got shit for your ass but hella harsh words and an attitude.

  I had learned a great many things from my comrades in the Black Liberation Army. Such would last me a lifetime. I had engaged in the pattern, tactics, philosophies, and history of those labeled as "imperialists" probably more than most would believe. I entered San Quentin and moved straight up the political ladder, yet was and have always lacked ambition. Just love for my people moved me. I know there would be some who'd find my shooting so-called pimps in their mouths and their so-called security guards in their ears so couldn't hear to be extreme. I also knew that many would be outraged at our setting Jezebels' pussies on fire, and would seek to throw the book at us for such. Notwithstanding, the pouring and squirting of lighter fluid and/ or gasoline in the ear of anyone deemed a real threat to our community would be met with pure rage. Perhaps even by our own immediate families, should they ever become cognizant that Vic and I, and sometimes others, were out and about doing such. Yet, I also knew my people, as with almost all people minus those who harbor the same mindset as people like me, would never take issue with the appalling deeds this government has and just plain continues to do. All the way down to Barack Obama. It hasn't and won't ever change. The masses don't know about deception, trickery at its highest level and, if you think what the brothers and myself from the 'tre did was so, so very outrageous, perhaps you should engage me in a historical dialogue and we'll explore what all has been done by whom everywhere they have gone.

Say what you will, but I am very aware of history. I am even more protective of my sisters first, and brothers, second. This because sisters reproduce us. Brothers cannot. It is very elementary. I will never stand around and allow any male to dog a sister and I'm able to do something about it. Lessons well taught indeed are lessons well learned. I refuse to apologize. Wish I would. If you are so concerned about females getting their pussy set on fire, don't stop there. Take it upon yourself to go and find out exactly where there fathers are. Why don't you track them down and hold them accountable for their biological daughters running around at all hours of the night? Allowed to step up to any car, van, station wagon, motor home, and any and everything else that comes her way, without question. While simultaneously, males galore stand on the street corners sippin' on this and that, and/ or sit in their cars listening to music, peeping out the rear-view mirror now and then to see what's jumping. Yet nobody ever steps up for the females and sides with them. The females are found in the city morgue clean smooth across this crooked-ass empire with no respite, 24/7/365, dead as hell. Killed. Murdered. Tossed in lakes and creeks. Found in alleys and abandoned buildings. The list goes on and on and on. Yet, if I try to get involved, no matter on what level, and it appears to call for drastic measures, I'm wrong. I'm mentally disturbed, mentally demented, mentally deranged and such. Newsflash: Not by a long shot. Fed up, not going for it, harbor the ability to peep erroneous deeds when I see such is my position. One of the many thinks I learned when I was in a safe-house with my BLA comrades, and I believe it was Comrade Assata who used to always say, "'Pend on who's measuring stick you use."

Be all as it may, I still remain vigilant of my sisters, and females in general, but nowhere near like I do for the sisters. We come first, come what may. I have a twin sister. How in the world could I stand around and let some punk-ass (I almost used to n-word) sit on his punk ass and con my sister into going out on the streets and let any human do anything they want for what, twenty dollars, give or take? Yeah, ok. All y'all just got to get mad at me b'coz I'm getting dude, Johnny-on-the-spot. Fuck him, his homies, his hood, fuck any and all pigs, fuck any and all so-called district attorneys, fuck each and every judge, individually and collectively, who would dare so much as cast "me" into a negative, problematic, violent light. Yeah, let y'all tell it. However, let ME tell it: y'all the ones a coward. And also let me add, GOOD! That's what y'all ass get for causing people like me who was minding own business. But no! Y'all allow males to do all kinds of shit...and get away with it. And your daughters be getting straight dogged out. Why you think folks coined the term "dog?" I, at least, get up off my ass and try, but naw, I'm the criminal. I'm the one who need to be locked up and all this. Let me make it clear: fuck you and your so-called death penalty. I could give less than a dam. If I see something wrong, especially something irrefutably wrong, like today—whiteboys calling whiteboys niggas, and Mexicans today (2011) calling Mexicans nigga, and brothers allowing 'woods and Mexicans to say it, use it, and even call them it, trying to justify it. "Aw, cuz is a white Crip. He from our hood. Done put mo' work in den dem other niggas." And/ or, "Aw he's a Blood, man. He done put major work in for the set. He down." So go the justifying, allowing different races to use the n-word. Then you can find Black gang members, especially Crips, who will allow a Mexican to call him nigga, but dare a whiteboy to even so much as be heard using it period. Think we might want to take a closer look at record companies, and perhaps we need to stop bullshitting and straight jam the record industry as a whole, straight out. I think I might have a tactic that would seeeeeriously not just get their attention, but force their hand to ban the n-word immediately.

Another thing, and seriously trip this, females: To all females, why is it you seem to gravitate towards known punks? Even kick-it with them, protect them, both on the streets and throughout the California prison system? Even FEMALE GUARDS, knowing these males are naught but

FEMALE IMPERSONATORS. But you same females, if you are to get pregnant and have a male-child, you will have a hissy-fit if the child is treated a certain way. E.g., if your "man" was to dress his and your son up like a sho'nuff sho'nuff female, a baby, an infant, or otherwise, you'd get at his ass. But it's ok if it's a so-called GROWN male to dress up in female attire. Disgusting. 'Nuff said about faggit ass punks and the folks who adore them. Suffice to say, mixed up ass muthafuckas!

It is 100% true that people tend to mock reality. That movie line "You can't handle the truth," I recall back in Folsom State Prison, the pigs there posted/ taped a picture of Brother Mujahid Abdullah (x-E. Grandberry) and myself on a beam, right in front of R&R, and it was conducted where the weather would not damage it. And they left it posted for all to see, for almost two years flat. At the bottom, someone had typed the following words in small but very dark, clear, bold print, "THESE TWO INMATES HATE THE WHITE RACE AND WANT THEM OFF OF THE PLANET!" We had to file paperwork and, only after running their gauntlet up to Sacramento, did they finally take it down. Let it be known that, just as Comrade George had confided in specific individuals that the odds were that he would not be alive to see his book *Blood In My Eye* printed, I say the same in regards to this one. To quote the Hon. Elijah Muhammad, "I know what you know not." And I said that to say this: I know that there exist those within this would be so-called prison administration (industrial complex) who want me dead. I know this to be a hard fact. Yet, also know, I'm anything but afraid. They've already stepped to me with cyanide (long before so-called lethal injection-ism). So, come with it. I'll never relent from speaking the truth. It would be my comrade Geronimo Pratt who gave me the name Kenyatta because of how I rep reality. It would be one of my Indian potnahs who felt what I wrote in support of his folk at Wounded Knee years ago. And he it was that stated the phrase, "Ashanti, you spit fire!" And, it sorta caught on. There was also a time right here in the so-called CDD (California Department of Degradation) that brothers used to call me Farrakhan because of how I used to give khutbahs (sermons) in the prison's so-called chapel/ make shift masjid. I was Imam for six years flat in the '80s. Such calls to mind when I gave just such a fiery sermon yester year, and the reaction I got. Check: First I decided to speak on and about "Ronald Reagan" and his endeavors to do away with "welfare." So I waited until Brother Mujahid Shabazz was finished—this was not the same Mujahid. Mujahid Shabazz is one of the so-called Zebra Killers from the

Bay. Mujahid Abdullah is from L.A., an ex-Crip turned freedom fighter. This brother speaking along with myself were elected to speak at the very first Black August ever held in San Quentin, where it was founded. When Brother Mujahid Shabazz finished his speech and I came up to the makeshift podium there on the Max-B yard, I greeted everybody, then started in on that ass. I stated, "I hope Ronald Reagan is re-elected. I also hope he actually do get rid of welfare, and that he continues to oppress, suppress, and repress the down-trodden to no end." As I figured, there were some brothers who immediately became visibly upset. One so much so he began to wave his hand frantically to speak. I acknowledged him and he commenced. "Ay, brother, you know, like, Ronald Reagan is no friend of the Black man. He constantly tightening the noose around our neck." On and on he went. I let him get his two-cents in. When complete, I replied, not just unto him, but everyone who had ears to hear. "That's what we need, brothers. More and more oppression. To be oppressed sooo much, until there is no choice but to stand up, unite for real, and eradicate the problem. In this case, the problem is the fascist-ass U.S. government. I gave a short spill about, "When someone feels strongly about something, they will eventually react."

I then proceeded to read a letter from Comrade George that I had always safeguarded. A brother comrade, yesteryear, entrusted it to me, along with transcripts of the San Quentin Six trial. The letter itself was actually written from a true to form comrade to Comrade George while he was in the so-called hole in O-wing suffering from various illnesses. One, life-threatening: his liver, which did usher in his demise after all. His name was Ulysses McDaniels. An absolutely dedicated brother if ever there was one. He was very close to my big homie and fallen comrade, W.L. Nolan. I grew up with Cornell and W.L.'s brother who was my age, Bud Nolan. We went to Castlemont together, and I once made the tragic mistake of selling Bud some catnip along with some real weed seeds Vic and I used to save when we bought weed back in the day. I sold Bud a matchbox of catnip for a nick (five dollars). Bad move. He doubled back and nutted up on me. That in addition to firing on me. Straight dropped me. We fought like Jews and Muslims in a phone booth. Afterwards, we became tight. Had crazy respect for each other's heart and nerve. Such is how I met Bud Nolan.

The letter was one of four written to Comrade George. It entailed a promise to never give up and never give in. McDaniels promised to always tell the truth and to always support people in the right. The entire content of this letter along with the oath was printed in the Black Panther newspaper on August 28, 1971, one week after Comrade George Lester Jackson was killed at San Quentin. The oath appears herein in its original form, no additions or omissions involved. The letter unto George ended thus:

> IF EVER MY WORD SHOULD PROVE UNTRUE,
> SHOULD I BETRAY THE MANY OR YOU FEW,
> THIS OATH WILL KILL ME.
> SHOULD I BE SLOW TO MAKE A STAND,
> OR SHOW FEAR BEFORE THE HANGMAN,
> THIS OATH WILL KILL ME.
> SHOULD I MISUSE THE PEOPLE'S TRUST,
> SHOULD I SUBMIT EVER TO GREED OR LUST,
> THIS OATH WILL KILL ME.
> SHOULD I GROW LAX IN DISCIPLINE,
> IN TIMES OF STRIFE, REFUSE MY HAND,
> THIS OATH WILL SURELY KILL ME

It would be Comrade W.L. Nolan who, after Comrade George shared Comrade Ulysses' letter with him, whom took it upon himself to write a constitution. This constitution would have been "snook" out of one prison into another for decades. Those who read its contents and agreed became more than just friends, more than just "tight." They became "family," a Family member, and this was for life.

All original BGF members had to meet set pre-requisites. Foremost, to become a family member, you had to have a life sentence. If a prospective brother was considered "righteous," but did not have life, he had to have at least one murder. If did not have such, he first would have to go and commit murder. In addition—and I do believe needless to say, yet I will—you had to be BLACK to become a member of the Black Guerilla Family. The BGF was **not** a gang. It began as a political entity to fight any wrongs inflicted upon brothers in prison, to teach and instruct brothers in what they perceived to be the right way to go. If a brother was gambling on ass, meaning he knowingly didn't have any money to pay should he lose, oftentimes the BGF would step in and inherit the debt. Afterward, the brother would-be-gambler most certainly would be approached by a BGF rep and informed that he now "owed" the Family. At some point he would be tapped on the shoulder with regard to the debt. It could, and often would, be paid in many ways, but never would sexual activity be employed. That was one of the mainstays the BGF was oh so strongly against. That, and any kind or form of oppression being employed, Black-on-Black or otherwise.

It would be almost one decade later before Weusi Agusti (Black August) would be born in San Quentin. Often, my brother-in-law, Salahuddin Al-Muntaqim (x-Freddie Tidmore), originally from Long Beach, would get at me to type various drafts. Brother Fati Yero—brother of the late Black Panther, Alprentice "Bunchy" Carter—is perhaps one of the most sincere and truly dedicated brothers you'd ever want to meet. Fati Yero (x-Kenny "Midnight" Carter) and I would become very tight, very quick. It would be Fati Yero and Comrade Sadiqi (x-Willie Stafford, r.i.p.), Brother Mafuholi (x-Michael Stover), Hashima (x-Michael Murdock), along with myself, who first initiated establishment of classes during yard time. We didn't force brothers to participate, although I will not say we did not use persuasion of sort. But the end most certainly justified the means. Brothers commenced to learn at a record pace. After some time elapsed, brothers began to look forward to "cranking up the machine," in which I was designated to call cadence! Each and every yard, rain, shine, sleet, or snow, we came out to the so-called Max-B yard. We greeted one another, discussed whatever might be noteworthy, got it settled or put on the back burner, and a relegated 'rade would be told when we were done, and he'd commence to holler, "Ten minutes. Ten minutes." This let everyone know we would become mobile in ten minutes. Brothers commenced to stretch and prepare to participate in "the people's machine." Even though I was up under the old guard, as it is called, I still associated with the New Man faction. "Five minutes. Five minutes," brotherman would call aloud. In time, we'd line up in two lines. I'd holler, "Machine in motion!" All present would respond with, "Machine in motion, sir!" and set it in motion. We'd run a fixed number of laps. When completed, we'd form rows and commence our exercise program which consisted of sit-ups, jumping jacks, knee-to-chest, chain breakers, various forms of arm rotations, side bends, stretches of sorts, running in place.

One of my homies directly from the same hood, Bro. Jasiri (x-Harold Benson) was the younger brother of Hodari (x-James Benson). Truly a good brother, Hodari. Both the Bensons are just a wee bit younger than me, but we've known each other since we were young. I was always super tight with Hodari, the more laid back of the two. Jasiri was the thinker, and we sometimes called him "the general." Sometimes, "Fidel." Otherwise we'd call him "Commander" because of the way he used to conduct his affairs. Jasiri would give birth to what became known throughout the California prison system as "the Jasiri Burpees." This exercise consisted of running in place, going down into a push-up position, doing a push-up, returning to vertical position and starting all over. In time, brothers honed it to perfection and added all sorts of new and far more rigorous means of doing Jasiri Burpees. Jasiri would get out and end up in the Feds. Him and my boy Hashima (x-Michael Murdock).

During the construction, brothers took it to task not to step on the Muslims' toes with regards to Ramadan. Great pains were present in regard to not giving B.A. the look of a copy-cat to Muslims. It was hammered and chiseled into something exclusively Black. If no other reason compelled us, certainly, upon research, we agreed unanimously that many good brothers and sisters fell in the month of August. June, too, but we focused on August because we lost Comrades George, Jonathan, and Khatari who had their lives snatch away in the month of August. Not only that, but many of us were in prison during the time we lost George (1971), and some of us were down and been down since the time period we lost Manchild / Jonathan (1972). And, of course, Bro. Khatari, who was allowed to bleed to death on the ground in the so-called Adjustment Center or AC, a super-foul ass hole right in the middle of San Quentin. I got the privilege to meet Comrade Khatari and his brother, Bukhari (Light Bulb). Light Bulb and I became sort of tight, despite his temper. I mean, after all, I also have a ridiculous temper my dam-ness.

During Black August, we wore something black, usually an arm band, until such time pigs got to trippin'. Yet we still wore something black on our person. We didn't listen to music, did not look at TV, and we most certainly didn't participate in the prison canteen for the entire month of August. We didn't eat nor drink anything from approximately 6 a.m. to 6 p.m. Brothers, especially comrades, were asked to endeavor to focus on the fallen 'rades and their sacrifices. To step up your studies and engage in study periods aside from the norm already established? No! We were concerning ourselves with a more intensified and elongated periods, that along with collective exercise being pushed to the max. Self-sacrifice, fortitude, and discipline were our main ingredients, and we cooked to perfection. The concept of revolutionary Black Nationalism was coming into being and being carried out right there inside the walls of San Quentin. Black Nationalist philosophy was at an all-time high in prison. Well did we know of yesteryear's misadventures when 31 men were killed in 31 days right there inside San Quentin. I knew these stories long before I hit the Q because of a first cousin on my father's side, Junior Grayton. He was out of Chicago, just like Comrade George. Junior Grayton was the founder of the Black Mafia right there in San Quentin. I recall vividly when he got out and my father (r.i.p.) went and picked him up. Guess who tagged along for the ride? Yep! Lil' ole me. This had to 1961 or '62. I am uncertain, but later, my big homie Cornell Nolan gave me all the info. He and Big Black Buddha (x-Earl Satcher, r.i.p.).

Black August was all good. Straight positive. We fasted to teach self-sacrifice, spiritual awareness, and strength. The physical part of fasting was to strengthen our bodies and prepare them to go without. In that, we can do without. The mental part of it was to strive for inner peace, practice self-denial, and to engage in massaging and training the mind. We knew that one can "think much clearer" with less food in his or her system. We were about protracted struggle, and I am proud to say I was a part of helping put B.A. together. Brother Mujahid (x-Larry C. Green) and I gave the very first speech there in San Quentin, in the so-called Max-hole.

It would be at the second B.A., while in the so-called hole there in San Quentin, that I'd announce myself as the world's first "Communist Muslim Socialist." I gave a rather lengthy speech of my interpretation of the events of the day and some of times past. By this point of my capture, I had begun to seriously hone my experiences and was coming into my own in so far as being able to articulate them well. I touched on the island-nation of Cuba, and how Fidel and company dealt the mafia a death blow. I gave the counter-revolutionary interpretation of the Bay of Pigs its permanent place right along with the Kennedy administration. All of them got dusted by Fidel 'nem. Mafia-run gambling and prostitution met their demise. Land was divvied up and extended unto people. Houses, apartment rent, phone, and electricity rates were quickly adjusted. I spoke at length about fairness now present as opposed to times past. I spoke about racism being crushed under foot and discrimination being put down. How equality was made law and enforced. Illiteracy was replaced by literacy, and we see today Cubans live longer than any people on the globe—something Europeans don't like to see in print.

I resurfaced all the teachings I had received when I was traveling with my comrades in the military fold of the B.L.A. I made mention of the irrefutable fact that Fidel's regime opened factories and work was manifest. Schools came forth, and town after town after town was not merely looked after, but fixed. Raw militias surfaced and skills along military lines were perfected. Arms of sort were made manifest and military training became commonplace. I hit up how Cubans overstood the meaning of "conquest" in its proper context. I drove home the point of how Mr. Oppression, his brother, Mr. Capitalist, right along with their first cousin, Mr. Opportunism, hurried up, peeped game, and got in the wind.[16] How could I be opposed to such established anywhere on this planet? Notwithstanding, they took in my Comrade, Assata Shakur. I am very partisan of such people and events. Thus I am pro-communist. With me, it was more like "Goo-o-o-o-o-d morning, mis-stir bol-sha-vic, goodbye, imperialist." The hell with good morning, Vietnam.

Each B.A., we learned, we grew, for if for nothing else, the BGF tended to watch the goings on in the world and didn't allow themselves to become straight-jacketed. Then too, one of its founders, W.L. Nolan, was certainly pro-Nation of Islam. Some BGF, from its inception, were pro-Islam and some were pro-Communist. Likewise, many are erroneous in their belief that, just because Comrade George was pro-Commie, all BGF are and must be. Wrong! As I said, people tend to mock reality, but Dracula must flee at the break of dawn. At any time, you could approach any number of BGF and might hear them engaged in topics galore. We knew of Gaddafi when he was Muhammad Gaddafi, because we made it our business to know. We were in the business of learning. From learning, we knew, came progress. And from progress is stability birthed. Libya, some three-times bigger than Texas, was declared in 1977 to be "a people's revolution," and oil was discovered in 1959. I knew much about the Communist philosophy and read even more still.

---

[16] Escaped/ fled the country.

And you can lay a safe bet we kept horrid misadventures of Attica alive, and it remains so to this very day. We had info passed down and passed on with regard to the Jonathan Jackson/ Marin County Courthouse misadventure of August 1970. It took me more than two years to talk Brother Ruchell Magee into coming out to the yard and speaking with the brothers—many of them youngsters—so that they might learn first-hand just exactly what took place in the van. He told us in vivid detail how the first shot struck Man-Child (Jonathan), and it was a shot that caught him directly in the chin. Then he went into detail of who did what: how Brother James McClain said, "We're not gonna make it, man," and then shit hit the fan. What many didn't know was that Ruchell hadn't left his cell other than to shower for some 14 years flat. He wouldn't do it. So, it wasn't easy at all to persuade him to come out and speak with the brothers. But it was certainly worthwhile in the end. Ruchell Magee, by far, is the bitterest person I've ever met in my entire life, bar-absolutely-none. He came, he spoke, he again disappeared.

In my time inside these walls, I met personally, face to face, Bill "Big Bear" Asher. Bear was once the photographer for some five years at Soledad Prison. Big Bear, as was the case all over the CDC, would come in and take the photos. This was actually the so-called "job description" convicts were allowed yesteryear. This was during the time the three brothers, Cleveland Edwards, Alvin Miller, and W.L. Nolan were gunned down. Bear laid it bare. He told me in vivid detail how all three brothers were shot in the back. All three translated into something. One, perhaps. But all three? No! And this because, when any incident jump off, guards yell, "Down on the yard!" Everybody within earshot knows to get down. If they are not within earshot, they can see other convicts get down, which automatically lets them know that something's up. If nobody else knows, I know pigs killed all three brothers. They had it out for W.L in particular. They murdered all three and, for a time, they got away with it. But unbeknownst, they had set some sho'nuff serious shit in motion. Shit that would last for decades and beyond. Black August would not, under no circumstances, allow a lid to be reattached to the can of worms that had been opened. It was opened and gonna stay that way come hell or high water. The learning process must (and did) continue.

We made it our business to let the masses know how shiesty the CDC is, and how they paid a settlement in 1983 to the families of W.L. Nolan,

Alvin Miller, and Cleveland Edwards. A damed shame, to say the least. Fifty-grand. Fifty chicken shit grand for the life of three brothers. And not just any ol' three brothers. These brothers were revolutionaries. I wasn't gonna be that easy. We made all with ears learn and hear about the political decree issued by Comrade George with regard to the life of any brother lost at the hands of the administration (i.e. guards), that it would cost them (guards) three for each of ours. We advanced brothers to stand up and speak, and speak clearly so that all could easily understand just what was being said and meant. I was asked to elaborate on my family's mental state after learning of George's death. I obliged and took it a step further. I cleared up the erroneous thoughts going around regarding Comrade George and the death of Brother James Carr, who once was George's celly way yesteryear. Many brothers don't know the real about many major events that have gone down, the death of James Carr is one such example. Many brothers were of the opinion that a "Mexican gang leader" actually killed Brother James Carr because he wouldn't join ranks with Man-Child (Jonathan Jackson, George's younger brother) and help him liberate the brothers going to trial in Marin. Brothers were found to be on the yard in Tracy Prison, Soledad Prison and Quentin, talking about the "Panthers" paid dude (a Mexican from the Nuestra Familia gang—a northern entity very highly organized and even more serious) to "off" Brother James Carr. The long and short of it is, I got it straight. I then took it to task to share the info. I had encountered with regard to George putting "dragan" (a hit on) Sister Angela Davis. Not true! George never put a contract out on Angie. Never happened. George did, however, put a contract out on any pig inside California prison walls that took a brother out. To adduce his seriousness, all of a sudden, a pig came up "discovered" dead. He would be discovered at night. He was officer John V. Mills. He was thrown to his death from the third tier in Y wing. We had been told his neck was broken all the way around. A note was attached to his body that read, "ONE DOWN, TWO TO GO!"

Shortly thereafter, another pig was offed. He, too, was discovered dead. He was William Shull, 40 years old. Found in the sports equipment shack of the north mainline yard. He had been stabbed 42 times. A note found attached to his body read, "TWO DOWN, ONE TO GO!" It took a lil' time for another hit to jump because of security concerns, the lockdown, and the time it took brothers to get and transform materials into weapon, get said in the need-be spot, and then get off. But it dam'sho jumped. The third officer was Robert McCarthy. His throat would be slit by a soldier from Nicaragua named Hugo Pinell. I gave it my best to impart knowledge and, after a while, I became known for offering up information. One day I would be transferred to Folsom and become tight with Hugo Pinell, whom we preferred to call Daha. We used to work out on the heavy bag together as well a jog. It really took some doing but, truth be told, if not for the BGF, a lot of erroneous info would be in the heads of brothers galore, especially the Bloods and Crips.

It would eventually come to pass that we worked our way around to Brother Geronimo Pratt. We had been made aware that his wife was found murdered, her body tossed on the side of a freeway, with a .38 stuck up her vagina. She was eight months pregnant. Brothers felt for Geronimo. And, being that he was once next door to me, that for a time we were both up on the row, that we used to go on visits together, and I met his current wife, Chaka, of course I didn't like it. We recently lost Brother-comrade Geronimo, but that's only in the physical. He will forever be in the minds and hearts of many. I know this to be true. Ji Jaga loves on. So we took it to task to spotlight all we could about Louis "The Rat" Tackwood. We most certainly shared all we knew with regard to the brothers up at UCLA and had their lives snatched. It was referred to as the BPP (Black Panther Party) vs. the U.S. (United Slaves), and the punk traitor and so-called founder of Kwanzaa, Ron Karenga. We seriously took issue with this brother and held him responsible for the deaths of both Comrades Alprentice "Bunchy" Carter and John Huggins, killed up at UCLA.

Now, I'm not tooting the horn of nor for the BGF. I am merely calling like it was and is. If for them, many events would have gone unknown or unchecked, and even more brothers would have been taken out than have already been. All thanks to the BGF. We fought for brothers (Blacks) when no other brothers would. This is a matter of record. Black August offered up the opportunity to set many records straight, and so, straight we set'em. There actually is no room to refute. It was we (BGF) who would first step to brothers with cultural awareness and suggested to commence using yard time for other than lifting weights and playing chess or dominoes. We started classes of sort. Not one or two. We put our best foot forward by selecting and or electing brothers that were best qualified, and they were charged with the responsibility of speaking on topics. They were to decree then collect and grade papers on those topics. No other brothers in the history of the CDC had done this but the BGF. Crips were never about studying. Later—much later in fact—they endeavored to surface the CCO (Consolidated Crip Organization) and it flopped almost straight from the gate. Reason being: no bona fide leadership. They (Crips) have never had a reputable leader minus Brother Raymond Lee Washington, whom I met in DVI/ Tracy right before he went home—only to be murdered by his own (Blacks). Shot gunned in the stomach and chest. Raymond (r.i.p.) was about studying, and he loved history, and desired to see the Crips organized. We walked and talked on the yard a number of times, Raymond Washington and Raymond Chapman both. Both, good brothers. Solid. Raymond Chapman became one of my personal potnahs at Tracy. A true gladiator he was. We rode together: me, him, Bad-habit Rabbit, Flan, Backarm Brown from the Vanguards, and of course, Jomo (Roosevelt Ducat).

It would be the BGF who explained in detail to the brothers the whys and the wherefores of the importance attached to a brother or sister changing their slave name. We took it to heart. I cannot take full credit for the application of brothers changing their slave names, but I was most certainly influential as I brought this concept with me from the B.L.A. It is without question, I gave more brothers cultural, Arabic, Swahili, Farsi, and Urdu names than any other brother in CDC history, bar none. In fact, no brother even comes close. People, I learned, tend to trip when a brother changes his slave name. They fail to realize that to us, a name is very significant, unlike others—save the Hispanic element—who didn't arrive here as we brothers did. Therefore, they have always retained their cultural names because their culture remained intact. Not the case with us brothers. Not by a long shot.

I remember when Malcom X changed his name? What jumped? Those of you who were around should remember. I dam'sho do. Them 'woods like to had a hissy-fit. Even worse so when Muhammad Ali changed his. 'Woods was like, "Whatta you mean you don't used Cassius anymore?" They couldn't get into it for shit. Remember how they tripped on Kareem Abdul Jabbar? Remember Keith Wilkes (basketball/ NBA player) and how he changed his name to Jamal? Folks like to went crazy. Chris Jackson, who went to LSU with Shaq, changed his name to Mahmoud Abdul Rauf and embraced Islam. He took it even further. During basketball games, he would not stand, let alone put his hand over his heart, when 'woods was having their—I reiterate, THEIR—so-called national anthem sung. They gave the brother the B.B. King blues for not standing for "their" national anthem. So, consequently, the BGF and I really took it to task to educate brothers. Any brother who has ever met me or even so much as encountered me for a brief period of time knows, all I do is spit real history and such. Knowingly, illiteracy is the enemy—arch enemy—of my people. Ignorance is the #1 enemy of my people. I see it, challenge it, and wage combat in various forms against it with some measure of success. Because of the sheer number of people alone, I remain one of the chosen few who yet combat ignorance, with hopes my efforts, deeds, and tactics one day will become contagious. I am often heard talking about and giving props to my brother, KRS-One, who was one of the first rappers to stand up and wage combat against ignorance. He didn't merely get a record deal and then turn heels. Bullshit. KRS stood up and hollered at his people. I can name tracks galore by him where he is endeavoring to wake up and educate his people. The track he did with Brother J from X-Clan, "Grand Verbalizer," how real is that! It is to be found on X-Clans CD *Return from Mecca*. Speaking of which, tell me X-Clan isn't a cut above the rest! They do not come more vicious than them. People need to trip KRS-One's track about whites calling whites niggas! Now, remember, he spoke on it way back in '95! Dam'sho did! Mad props and respect unto you, Brother KRS-One. Nothing but big ups to you and X-Clan.

Like any entity, the BGF has made mistakes along the way. So we learn to proselytize more efficiently and forever be on the lookout for illiterate brothers. Some of us, after the 1979 Islamic revolution in Iran (Persia), sometimes used on the clandestine tip the word "Ayatollah" (sign of God) because the true BGF has for the longest known that the BLACK MAN IS GOD. "WE" know who we are. So in 1977 a political decree was issued saying that ALL BGF would embrace a cultural name, like it or not.

One of the most trying episode for me since I was captured would have to be in 1981. I would be transferred from San Quentin to Folsom. Folsom was entirely different than San Quentin. In '81, I was approached by some brothers who asked me to at least try to organize something. One of the brothers was a truly dear comrade of mine, Shilo (z-Herbie Thurman). Shilo and I grew up together and my twin sister used to be very fond of him. He was always a womanizer and I used to tell him a great many times, "The BGF isn't for you, brother." But...

I listened to brother comrade, and I clearly understood the relevancy attached. Shilo had just gone to the feds to do time. When I saw him again, it was unbelievable how much he had changed. Back in Oakland he was always known for fighting. From junior high on up, Shilo would fight anything that moved. Now in Folsom, he quickly became known for puttin' hands on whoever for using that infamous n-word, or worse still, calling sisters that dreaded b-word. Shilo wasn't having it, he became the standard-bearer against it. Bet not hear a Crip or some youngster who habitually uses the so-called n-word. Ma-a-a-an. Shilo was for certain fixing to jam him! Absolutely no doubt. I became very impressed with my homie Shilo and his remarkable change. So, I accepted his suggestion and commenced to get at various people with regards to establishing an event.

It would be directly in regards to what was jumping in Atlanta, Georgia. A brother, slave named Wayne Williams, had been arrested and charged with killing a great number of Black children over a considerable amount of time. Many, many young Black brothers and sister were being found slain. Oftentimes thrown in a river. The brother, Wayne Williams, would be arrested and charged with hella murders, but the exact same murders were still jumping off regularly as he sat in some Atlanta county jail waiting to go to court. Sister-mothers were just having fits because all of a sudden they began complaining when their offspring were found that, "That's not my child!" or "My baby has been messed with!" Come to find out, after so much "noise" was being made, Brother Dick Gregory, and later the mighty Nation of Islam, got involved. Dick Gregory went on a fact finding mission in Georgia. Yes indeed, Black folk, the following information was printed in newspapers, and I myself once had a copy. But going to and fro, in and out of the so-called hole, much property was taken and/ or I was made to send it home. I once obtained newspaper articles by the Nation of Islam headlining, "Sister-mothers in Atlanta are not saying the dead body of this child and that child is not theirs," or, "The body has been 'messed with.' When asked what these sister-mothers meant when they employed the term 'messed with,' unanimously, they said that their 'private parts' had been tampered with." It would later be learned that these same children that had "gone missing" and later found floating in the river—or worse—were said to have a "puncture wound" at the base of their skulls. The theory was advanced by Brother Dick Gregory and the Nation of Islam that the "Germans" had invented something called "Gamma Rays" that created and emitted rays. These rays came from a miniature umbrella-looking device and, when pointed at humans, caused them to become unconscious immediately, and this is how so, so many of our children were coming up missing and never any form of fight seen or screams heard. All this while Brother Wayne Williams still sat in the so-called county jail, right there in Atlanta. No form of protest was ever mounted on the brother's behalf. Absolutely no noise. No one came to the brother's aid whatsoever. Yet murders committed in the exact same way he was said to have done were still jumping off on the regular, and in the exact same area. When children were found while Wayne Williams was still sitting behind bars, with absolutely no one making any kind of noise, it behooved some, including my Comrade Shilo, to address the situation. So much so, I was able to organize any brother on the line that wanted to come to the prison church to listen, learn, and speak on what was going on in Atlanta. I organized the event, set a date, got with and made recommendation to each brother who planned to speak, and they agreed with the suggestions. When the date came around, it was on in the worst way. We set it off and let folks have it.

I even attempted to establish contact with the TV program 60 Minutes, concluding that, after all, they had my case on their show. Dam'sho did, but they refused to answer my kite (letter). I wrote a very sincere, humble, and forthright missive. To no avail. Eventually, Brother Wayne Williams was convicted, and off to so-called prison he went, almost without a peep. My position ever since has been this...and let it he heard and know in each and every goddam city: FUCK ATLANTA!

This so-called government gets away with what they do simply because the masses are either too ignorant or too afraid to raise up and do something about it. I say here again, this government and this prison system want me dead. Let it be known.

"They are going to kill me, they are gonna murder me." "I don't think they would, given your visibility," Johnny replied.

"The obvious," George replied, "is often the most overlooked." Johnny went on to say, and I quote, "The guards hate George even more now that his best-selling book[17] had focused outsiders' attention on the racist treatment of Black prisoners. As a result of his allegations, the Marin County Grand Jury was now investigating prison conditions."

---

[17] *Blood in My Eye*

"George explained to Johnny how a few month earlier, a white prisoner, Alan Mancino, had filed an affidavit in court saying that prison officials had threatened to kill him unless he killed George Jackson. They had told Mancino, 'We don't want another Eldridge Cleaver.'"

I employed this from my boy Johnny Spain's book totally without permission because we are just that tight. We did time together and we were even going to escape while at Tracy. We mapped it out but it was foiled because my father passed away. Johnny was allowed to come visit me in the hospital during lockdown on May 5, 1979, after whiteboys attacked me. All nine of them had knives. Johnny and I were also on the same basketball team, and we won a trophy there at Tracy. I don't believe he would mind me quoting from his book, *Black Power, White Blood: The Life and Times of Johnny Spain* (by Lori B. Andrews), not one bit. And he still can't beat me playing basketball.

From my celly Charles Captain, murdered in punk-ass San Quentin, to my lil' potnah, the Crip Tony Sewell (aka Herk or Hurk), who hung himself as I slept, and to the many stabbings I witnessed, and in some cases had to do my dam-ness, it is no wonder why people ask me why I "always" wear shades. Only a very few can say they have seen my eyes, something I learned from my celly who was murdered right before my very eyes. He, as well as my twin sister, always commented about my eyes, saying they have the most evil look they have ever seen. I don't know, maybe so. Some say my eyes look like burning fire, and my reply is that it's from lack sleep.

My throat is parched from talking constantly to the young. I especially target those who have action at getting out and make them very aware and instruct them to "share this information." That at any time, this government can turn any "Safeways" or "Lucky's" or any other so-called supermarket into a federal holding facility within 25 hours if warranted—in their opinion. This translates into a prison. Know and understand people. The only reason why nab Jones (that name for police my father used to love to use and I got it from him), have not done such with these "occupiers"[18] is simply because they pose no real threat to the security of this empire. I prefer, actually, to refer to AmeriKKKa as a corporation because that is actually what it is.

---

[18] Occupy Wall Street, etc.

So, I look this way, speak this way, carry myself this way, and say what I say because, maybe like Comrade George, I too have blood in my eye!

ISLAM

I began flirting with Islam in 1974. Of course I had come in contact many times as a youth on the streets of Oakland, but paid little to no attention. It wasn't "rowdy" enough for my liking. Boy oh boy did my reading, studying, and research here in prison hurry up and changed my views! Here in prison, I came across the words of Malcom X:

"THE WORST MISTAKE THE WHITEMAN

MADE WAS TO SEND ME TO PRISON,

THE LEARNING CENTER OF THE UNIVERSE."

When I read those words by Malcolm, they stopped me dead in my tracks. Ponder was the word. And ponder I seriously did. I knew I was captured and in prison, I knew I certainly wanted (and needed) to learn, and the words stirred something up in me that I was uncertain about. One thing about me, I have always just loved to learn. And, I have always loved Black females. They were my world. I can say with pride, I am yet to ever so much as lay a finger on a sister. Never have, never will. Pops taught his son far better than that. Fuck popular opinion. I dig Brother E-40, even have some of his music, but I don't like his track "Captain Save-A-Ho."

I can say that all my life I have been exposed to some very strong Black brothers and sisters. Aunts, uncles, cousins, associates, and people I didn't become annexed to but just got to know through introduction. Some, at a certain junction in my life, happened to be Muslim. Take for example Brother Cornell Nolan. The effects of what that brother taught me and exposed me to at that particular time of my life was truly outstanding and devastating to my young mind. "The Black man is GOD!" "The white man is the devil!" Yeah, he had my full undivided attention, and then some.

However, it would be in prison where I truly began to do my own studying. Later I would begin researching, and later still I entertained cross-referenced research. The entirety of history was before me. I dove into the likes of H.G. Wells' "Outline of History," volumes one and two. I ran through all of Brother J.A. Rogers' works. I devoured everything in my path. Far too much and many to begin to enumerate. Moreover, my comrades out in Los Angeles would, of all things, open up a book store. Sho'nuff thanks to my brother, Imam Muhammad Abdullah and Comrade Zaid of Zaid's Dawah Book Shop. They sent me some of everything. In time, this would enable me to independently study all schools of thought within Islam. I ate up everything I could get my hands on along the Sunni school of thought. Hadiths, Fiq, and all manner of Islamic jurisprudence. I sponged it up. Probably even worse when I collided with the al-Shi'ites. Al-Kitab (the book) "Najul Balagha" (Peak of Eloquence) by Imam Hazrath Ali seriously blew me away. I sent for more literature and received it. I started to correspond with people in Sudan, Egypt, Morocco, Indonesia, and China. There are a great number of Muslims in China. I didn't know that—but I do now. I wrote to and began corresponding with people from everywhere and with anybody. It didn't matter. I'd write them if they wrote me. Likewise, I wrote to each of the Christian ministers here in the states. I would purposely and punctually get up, with pen and paper in hand, waiting for John Hagee, Oral Roberts, and any and all other ministries that were televised yesteryear. All of them. I didn't discriminate. Pat Robertson and I kicked it for the longest. I was able to secure correspondence with people in the 700 Club. I received literature from some of everybody. I engaged in classes so that I might obtain credentials of sort. I simply wanted to KNOW! Nobody was out of reach. If they existed on this planet, I'd somehow exhume their mailing address and jot them some words. Many, but certainly not all, wrote me back. Some, as said, lasted for a very considerable amount of time, and unto each I am eternally grateful.

One of the most unique experiences I had was when my 'rade and mentor, Imam Muhammad Abdullah of Compton, California went to Asia and made Hajj (pilgrimage), and from Saudi Arabia he traveled to some of everywhere. In Sudan he established contacts and information which I still carry to this day. He went to al-Medina and sent me some of the most B.O.M.B. greeting cards you'd ever want to see. Totally colorful and unique. In addition, he travelled to the Islamic Republic of Iran (Persia) for a minute. In Iran he met the Revolutionary Guard and various other people. Imam Muhammad was blessed to actually have dinner with the president of Iran and the esteemed Imam Ayatollah Khomeni. During their dialog Muhammad made mention of some brothers here in the snakes (so-called United States) that met p.o.w. and political prisoner status. He extended our names and provided them information on how to go about writing us.

In my opinion the most important thing Muhammad accomplished was when he was escorted to the frontlines where Iran and Iraq were fighting. There, Imam Muhammad talked to many mujahideen. He spoke of brother freedom fighters here in the snakes and endeavored to explain that our fight at the present time was far different than freedom fighters elsewhere. After explaining how the great satanic whore, AmeriKKKa had locked away (warehoused) most freedom fighters for one reason or another, and the mujahideen fully understood, some of them would go on to write me a book—a complete book—from right there on the front lines, in the trenches fighting Iraq. They would actually dip their index finger in a fallen comrade's wound and write in English as best as possible on whatever possible, bind the material together mostly through a piece of thread, and mail it to me via one of the mujahidin's wives. Amazingly, Folsom allowed it in. I got it. I read it several times over before I commenced to take it out and allow others to get a bar. It moved many of the brothers so much so that often, some within the rank and file of the BGF, many Crips, and Bloods too, all decided to join ranks with me as I announced my intention to start a new ikhwanul Muslimeen (Muslim brotherhood). BGF became very hostile with me and accusations flew. Tensions were born and there were talks time and again about what should and should not be. I decided to push on with the agenda I had in mind.

I was able to pull from each entity some of their best. Certainly some of their brightest thinkers and frontline soldiers. Far and away the most bona fide brother I pulled would be Brother Mujahid. At that juncture, he was on the so-called Crip yard under the CCO machine. Every day he would come to fence that separated our yards and call me. We'd talk and I'd listen to him very closely. He was very passionate. Absolutely nothing reactionary about him. He was forever willing to learn as he asked me more questions than a D.A. Again and again he'd say, "The next time I go to committee, I'm going to have them put me over there on the yard with you." And he did exactly that. We became tighter than tight. We quickly built a brotherhood from scratch. Our first recruit would be Brother Ajene Yero, one of the most serious brothers you'd ever wanna meet. He once took a billy club from a female pig and whooped her and her partner during shower time because she insisted that he "strip out." All of us had had yard meetings and decided we would NOT engage in stripping out in front of a female, come what may. He beat her and him, male and female pig, like he had a license. Ajene was devout. Wasn't into playing games. Didn't say much, but when he did, he was straight to the point with no chaser. We pulled Ajene Yero. Next we set our eyes on a young blood approximately 25 years old. We could see soldier in him from afar. His slave name was Michael Green, soon to become known throughout California and beyond as Malik Abdullah. Now if you think Comrade Ajene Yero was quiet, Malik was super quiet. Very healthy, and an awful good listener. Coupled with total loyalty, Malik would be our next one to be sponsored into our jamaat (group). We then set our sights on another brother. This one was out of East Oakland. We all knew he bore watching just by the things he did, let alone what all he'd day in the yard-meeting type situations. As was the case with each and every one of the brothers mentioned up to this point, I gave each a new name, one in keeping with their character and all that I had come to know about each brother individually. This brother I gave the name Ramzadin! And he was something else too. It was seen throughout the yard we shared with the BGF. It was some 32 BGF at that particular time, and at that time we Muslims were only five deep. Our study ethics left absolutely nothing to be desired. We conducted our affairs like no one else before nor after. Now all of a sudden, all eyes were on us. At first the "New Man" faction of the BGF endeavored to impose their will on us. Not happening. We were too committed and it was soon discovered that we were not into some mere fad, nor was this hardly an "adventure!" We meant business, and it was fast becoming the new force to be reckoned with.

All of this occurred, for the most part, right smack-dab in the middle of a war between the BGF and the Mexican Mafia. The Mexican Mafia (EME) are from Los Angeles, mostly East L.A. They are deep numerically, very highly organized, with a unique history. This war started due to BGF members going out to L.A. for court. While there, they (two BGF members) engaged in an act of oppression. They assaulted a Mexican. Beat him down, took his tennis shoes, and endeavored to put him under a bunk. Caused him to have a pin put in his hip and walk forever with a pronounced limp. This was not just any Mexican, either. He was actually a fully functioning member of the EME. Once the two brothers had done their part in helping another individual at trial, they were returned back to the CDC. Things were business as usual for a good moment. That is, until the Mexican guy ran the gauntlet at court, went through Chino (a reception center) and ended up smack-dab in Folsom. This was "old Folsom," for at that time there was no such thing as "new" Folsom. It hadn't been built yet. The new building at Folsom wouldn't be built until '86.

Truth be told, and I know this for a fact, the Mexican that was assaulted in the L.A. County Jail, upon seeing the two brothers that did him the injustice while going to court, immediately reported them to his people. The EME approached us, the BGF. They would talk and talk to the then commander of that particular line, Chino. A complete, sporadic brother from Pasadena. Highly disliked by the New Man faction. To the extent that I had brought along with me from San Quentin a kite with regards to him, and it was also I who brought the C.O.E. to Folsom in 1981 from Quentin, sho'nuf sho'nuf, Chino would be removed only by military means. He was stabbed in the neck and found lying by the boxing ring by a sister pig. Chino would be rushed to the hospital and saved. All known BGF were removed from Folsom's mainline and locked up in the hole. A "new" day was dawning for real and fo'sho, and not just at Folsom. New Man had arrived and was thriving like it was the thing to do. I witnessed their birth and growth all the way to this point in time. And as I've stated, many are good brothers. I came into the family as one of the original cast and that's what and how I've always remained.

    New Man clashed with us here and there but, for the most part, they left us alone. Just as the New Man grew, al-ikhwan (the brotherhood) also grew. A war was brewing at Folsom. This was became so intensified that, in time, it spread not only throughout the entire CDC but also over and onto the streets. Brothers and southern Mexicans went at it. All this over two brothers sodomizing a Mexican. After the EME came to the BGF and requested we remove the brother who had been part of the injustice (the other one was not at Folsom, at least not at that time), the leadership under Chino Thomas outright refused to militarily discipline the brother. This put not only the BGF at risk of war, but also any brothers who were known to associate and/ or sympathize with them to any degree. We engaged in yard meeting after yard meeting trying to conclude the best option available. If we didn't "hit," the brother deemed responsible, EME would, and that would not be accepted by the BGF. The deadline given by the EME was upon us. Eventually, it arrived. The EME, true to form, wasted no time. They straight blasted brother and also hit another brother tier tender (new to prison) right in front of the visiting room. Oh, it was on fadamsho now. The war started in 1981 in Folsom and went on until 1987. Much blood spilled. We lost, they lost. Police at Folsom were openly betting about, "who'd win the war overall." For some five years we were consumed by this war. Convicts lost their wives and girlfriends. Sons hella young grew up peeping their pops forever in the hole for something or other to do with violence, his mother always upset during and after each visit. Many of those same youngsters are now in their 20s and are to be found here in prison, just as Brother Ice Cube described in his cut, "Lil' Ass G."

Things became so intense that eventually Crips became involved, too. The Bloods, always a close ally of the BGF and brothers from up north in general, had been in it straight from the gate. Especially the United Blood Nation, or UBN. There in Folsom for quite some time, they were visibly tight with the BGF. Now, three entities were directly in the war against the EME who also had the entire southern cartel (numerous as they were, and still are) backing them. It had become absolute chaos. Anything could (and often did) happen at any time to anyone. If they were caught slipping. Such is how the EME killed Brother Majaribu (Frisco Red, x-Richard Benjamin). Maja, as we called him, wasn't even Family. A sympathizer, yes. A gang member, no. I took it to heart and reported to my sho'nuff potnahs/ Comrades Lumumba and Faruq, "Look, brothers, I'm not gonna allow them Mexicans to get away with smoking Maja. First chance I get, I'm downing one of them. I suggest you both not exit your cage until such time you both have completed manufacturing a bone crusher. When done, holla. In the mean and in between, do not be heard on the tier. Do not employ Swahili unless absolutely warranted because, as you know, the Mexicans have been purchasing Swahili dictionaries for a good while now. Circumvention in terms of covert diction will be our mainstay. We must seriously employ tenets of the *Art of War* and inveigle these dudes. Be mindful, and keep ya thinking caps on. Ttf-A." Ttf-A meant or was a coded way some signed a kite that meant "True to form, Ashanti."

When my weapon was prepared, I didn't wait nor hesitate. I faced the east like some you may remember Muhammad Ali used to do in the ring before a fight. Well, that's exactly what I did. When done, I waited. The first Mexican I saw, I took off on. He was Edwardo Bjarno. Being escorted by two pigs to a committee hearing. I blasted dude in the side and he stumbled and yelled simultaneously. The next blow caught him high in his back and he fell. Alarms were the word. I dropped my knife, put my hands behind my back, and froze. I was handcuffed and escorted back to ad-seg. The story of my life. Twice I took flight on the Mexicans for the death of Brother Majaribu. It was strange. I had just got a bag of sour cream and onion chips from Maja for the game that night. Dr. J dam'sho won his ring that night. I didn't get to enjoy the game and I dam'sho didn't get to enjoy them chips. I was miserable. Such is life, I'd learn. Majaribu, r.i.p.

From my viewpoint, the BGF was constantly turning out to be more and more reactionary. Excuses were being made to "hit" brothers. Something I took strong issue with. All the more so after they hit Comrade Daha (x-Hugo Pinell), one of the original San Quentin Six members. I received letters from Marion and Joliet prisons, as well as from Attica, asking what's up with that. "What you brothers doing out there, killing off the remainder of those true to form?" I showed these kites to my 'rades PJ and Haazim. We walked and talked. But, in the eyes of many, the damage had been done. Family was now considered a social outcast. I had two comrades from the BLA fly in. They flew out here to Oakland from New York, met with BGF reps, dialogued, and departed. They concluded, "These brothers are straight reactionary, Brother Ashanti!" They flew back to New York, never to return to California.

In 1986, at the behest of CDC staff because of the pressure from Sacramento, a peace treaty initiative was manifested. It took some doing. The entire prison would be closed on the days when BGF and EME would be allowed out to meet and talk, both on separate sides of a cyclone fence. They would walk and talk, walk and talk. Finally an agreement was reached, and staff—not everybody, but especially STAFF—was happy. Folsom staff agreed that if we allowed six from each side (six Black/ six Mexican) out of the hole and onto the mainline without incident, they (staff) would release six more from each side per week—minus incident—until all members were out of the hole. Such is how the BGF and EME got back in the mainline at Folsom.

I took the opportunity to grow. From out of the hole came brother Comrades Mujahid, Malik, Ramzadin, and me. We veered and embrace the Shi'ite school of thought for about four years now. We studied like truth seekers and zealots do. Once out, we went to work. First we obtained weapon stock, just in case. Remember now, we're in the CDC. Shit happens. Next, infiltrate. Peep the Sunnis and see what they were working with. A brother from Chicago (Muhammad) was acting as their imam. He was steppin' to brothers in the Brotherhood, asking them on the down low, "Do you get high? Between you and me, I got some hop (heroin). Wanna get loaded? If you do, you gotta keep it between you and I!" If the brother answered in the affirmative, Muhammad would go directly to the pigs and point the brother out in front of anybody in broad daylight. "Sir, that brother right there 'round here saying he's a Muslim, but messing with heroin. We don't want a brother like that a part of our brotherhood. Remove him off the mainline. He has some heroin on his person right now." Shit like that. So, initially, Brother Mujahid and I didn't believe it. Until we ran an old San Quentin tactic called "Good as Gold" on him, and Muhammad bit. Once confirmed, we voted and decided to remove dude from the line in Folsom. So, we did. Smooth as butter, we played him. We decided not to kill him. Instead just fuck him up to the point where all got the message that snitching would not be tolerated. We smashed Muhammad. There were very few rambunctious encounters from that point on as far as the Muslim brotherhood was concerned. Each brother who was neophyte knew the business.

Soon, a substantial number of the BGF became interested in annexing with us, knowing that what they were involved in was now merely a gang. Nothing militant of revolutionary about it. Brothers left the BGF. This, notwithstanding the outright murder of my sho'nuff boy, Haki Hodari Kambon (x- Eddie Glen Brooks), a brother I grew up with. His mother and my mother used to ride to work together at Del Monte cannery in Oakland. Haki and I would receive a visit the day before he was stabbed to death by the reactionary faction of the BGF. During the visit, Haki asked me point-blank, "Bra, have you heard anything about them brothers plotting to take off on me?" I told him, "Naw, bra. If I did, you know I'd say something. You know that man." We talked over by the Coke vending machine. His girl and my wife had caught the Greyhound up to see us. The murder of Haki Hodari seriously affected my wife, Jamilah. She was never really quite the same after that. Before Haki's murder, I had sent her to visit a comrade in Tracy. My 'rade Natural (x-Michael Stephens), a good for-real soldier. No question about it. He was strictly business. Jamilah visited him and returned with the needed info. Natural, who would later be transferred to Vacaville, took issue with a fag cutting in front of him in line during dinner and slapped him. The whiteboys refused to accept such and put the 'wood fag up to stabbing my boy Natural. He caught Natural coming down the stairs on the way to a visit. Natural apparently never expected the 'wood fag to get off, but that's exactly what he did. One shot, straight to the heart, and Natural tumbled down the stairs, dead. His mother and sister, Pepper, were waiting in the visiting room. The visit never took place thanks to a fuckin' punk!

So, the death of Haki was devastating to Jamilah. As for Haki's queen, she had to actually be put in a mental institution. Best believe I care! Hell, yeah. That was some cold shit. Haki was a bank robber back when you did fed time for bank robberies, this time he was in state due to the death of attorney Fay Stender who was once Comrade George Jackson's attorney. Haki and others believed she sold George out and gave information to the feds. Haki told me the entire get down from the giddy-up. In any event, he would be convicted for Fay's murder and sent to prison. In short, Haki became disgruntled at the BGF for stabbing Brother Daha (Hugo Pinell). A move that was felt, met with disdain and outcry from every quarter, as Daha had done nothing but sacrifice his very life and freedom for the revolutionary ideas of the chosen few, namely George, Huey, and Eldridge. Daha should have never been assaulted. Haki either. Even if Haki should not have done what he did to Fay Stender, he shouldn't have been attacked and murdered like that in Folsom's so-called "4-A"; a hole like San Quentin's Adjustment Center, or AC. Haki was killed the very next day after we had lost Brother Marvin Gaye. How much more death of good brothers we gonna cause, y'all? I veered towards Islam to see what it could possibly bring. Before it was said and done, the once famous, now infamous, BGF would stab my main man Mujahid in the neck while he was in the shower. The stabbing was so vicious Brother Mujahid lost the ability to speak for dam near two years. His vocal chords had been ruptured. I would be approached by the mighty east coast Crips lead by Big Sad, a major factor in the east coast Crip gang faction. I was asked to organize a move on the reactionary faction of the "new" BGF. The east coast Crips took it to heart that the reactionary BGF had the nerve to hit a bona fide brother like Mujahid who was one of their best, and if nothing else, certainly their brightest. In fact, there should be no argument if and/ or when it is ever said that Mujahid is not only the sharpest to come from the east coast Crip gang, but also the sharpest Crip turned freedom fighter of them all. I would have to say in all fairness, Sanyika Shakur (x-Monster) from Eight-Tre comes in second.

Together, Brother Mujahid and I built a jamaat unlike any other in the history of the entire CDC. We decided to become cellies, and from that point, it was on. We did the dam thing, fa'sho! It became commonplace when you seen Brother Mujahid, you saw me. When you saw me, you saw Brother Mujahid. We were not no ying and yang. No! We were both alpha males. Both leaders. Fearless, and harbored the ability to recall nearly anything we came in contact and able to recite it back without complication. Perhaps the flipside of that, the CDC had learned such with regard to him and me. An endeavor would surface to separate us, permanently if possible!

A quick word. Before I could finish this chapter, someone I knew just up and died on me. He was once a fully functioning member of the American Nazi Socialist, of ANS! We used to walk and talk and kick it about some of everything, not just prison. Arguably the best jailhouse lawyer here. He suddenly died. He truly left the ANS philosophy behind and moved on. Just wanna say, REST IN PEACE, JOHN!

Daaammmmn!

Chapter 9
Closing Arguments

"To blame a person
Who has truly changed
Is to blame a person
Who no longer exists"

(Jesus)

SOCIALISM

So-cial-ism: A theory of social organization based on government ownership, management, or control of the means of production and the distribution and exchange of goods.

So-cial-ist

(Merriam-Webster)

As I advance in age many things have now become clear to me. As a child, I always heard elder Black folk say something about the whiteman to the effect of them expecting us to "stay in our place." I now fully understand why many organizations have sprouted, although many if not most are defunct, they surfaced to wage combat over this "stay in your place," or "know your place kneegar" type shit. Pops used to always say, "Once you get it, can't nobody take it away!" He of course was talking about knowing the real and being cognizant of just exactly what's what.

The whiteman and race truly hate an educated brother, sister, or organization. They'd rather see me in a state of mind where I am predictable. In so far as youth are concerned, Nab would certainly rather see a gang of "knee-gars" with their asses all out and under the influence of something or other, than to come across a group that is quiet, acutely alert, bright-eyed, orderly, with just one person speaking while the remainder have their heads dropped, viewing a book. And this, mind you, is not in some classroom. No! This is on some street corner. This is in some residential park, minus gun play and violence of any sort. This is at the local gym, this is right outside, and in fact, up against a fast food spot. Lo and behold, brothers are up and studying, not to mention that this has been habitual. They can be seen in the same spots, and in fact, have been for months now with no hint of a problem, disunity, loud or embarrassing behavior that their race, indeed their parents, would be ashamed of. Nostalgia? Perhaps. Probable? Highly unlikely, but yet and still very possible. How do I know this? Because we Black Panthers of yesteryear did it all the time. You could roll up and there would be any number of us reading up on some of everything. With us not showing our ass cracks and letting our dress code dry snitch on us, ole' Nab didn't know what to make of us so he commenced to guess. When one has to guess, what does that say? Does it not say they are uncertain? When one is certain, they don't have to guess. When you guess, what oftentimes occurs? Mistakes. When you are educated, Nab don't' know what you are up to nor what you may do.

They don't know what to expect. They can't ever say with any degree of certainty just exactly what the brother, sister, or group will do. Like nations are purposely erroneously labeled, so be the case with us. We too are victims of false imprisonment. That is to say, we have been imprisoned in a lie. Those of us that sought enlightenment with success, these souls are called "ROUGE!"

I know that, to many, I have done much wrong. Some may label me a so-called serial killer, or worse. I am but one thing: serious. Serious about my love for my race. I want an even or level playing field for all. Seriously and without deviation, I want to see equal justice. Everything 50/50. How is it some have reached what are commonly called millionaire and billionaire status while other folks live on and off the streets? I mean, word?! Folks have so much shit they don't even know what all they have. Patty Hearst, for example, knew this. If she didn't know anything else, she knew her father had soooo much land that her and the S.L.A. could hide out on it and never been seen or detected. This is where they hid for the most part. Her father had "somehow" accrued so much land that it is actually a city in terms of sheer size. How does one person, male or female, come to "own" such an enormous amount of property? Think Randolph Hearst ever did any dirt? Need I name other woodchucks that so-called own property galore? J. Paul Getty, 'nem? Howard Hughes? The list goes on. Newsflash! Ain't that much hard work in the world! In fact, no person can work so many hours in their lifetime that they earn—and I purposefully reiterate EARN—billions! Knock if the fuck off.

Should a person such as myself, and other with a mindset like mine, begin to ask questions, we are fast labelled as a threat. I talk to correctional officers quite often. One, the gang lieutenant, told me flat out, "You know, Jackson, the Hearsts are gonna come after you with everything they got!" My reply was that I expected as much. However, if any Hearst so happen to read this book, hear me well and remember this if you don't do nothing else:

1. You have money. I am more than willing to undergo a polygraph test. Are you, Patty? Are you willing to pay for such a polygraph test, Hearst family?
2. In addition, I am completely willing to undergo hypnosis. I am willing to allow any person on the planet who is experienced in

      hypnosis to endeavor to hypnotize me and let's see what surfaces. How about you, Patricia? How about you, Hearst family?
3. In addition to the above, I am also willing to be administered any form of truth serum. I have heard about the Germans and how they have now perfected such. I am willing to be injected with any form of truth serum reputable in the scientific community. What say you, Tonya—I mean—Patty? What say you, Hearst family? How bad do you want to know the truth? Exactly. That's what I thought. I'd like to think veracity is paramount.

    Like with political assassinations, erroneous deeds birth questions. Knowing this, the rich cannot stand to be under the spotlight. The real may just come shining through. Yet Dracula MUST flee at the break of dawn. Me, I said it before and I'll say it again: I grew up around nothing but sho'nuff reputable thinkers. I yet speak on my boy Huey oh so much, and also of Eldridge. He and I were not cellies that long, but during the time we were, he really poured out his true inner feelings about many things. We certainly talked about the "power of words" a lot, and one word he liked to use was "sojourn." Eldridge had at some point in time been a part of some of everything. Almost every organization. If he hadn't joined it outright, he most certainly studied their philosophy. Moreover, he simply loved to chop it up. We would kick it deep into the wee hours the entire time we were cellies. Short lived as it was, two others and myself assaulted Eldridge Cleaver after receiving word from Huey that "Eldridge is going to testify against the party!" We ran in the cell on him as we had done many others in Oakland's county jail. In hindsight, we were wrong. There were so many ideologies afoot that, young me, I was torn. A mental straight tug-o-war.

    I really loved to hear the "Nation" speak. They showed absolutely no love for the whiteman, at least from a podium position. Then along came the "Zebra Killers!" They were four in number, had the same attorney I did, although I was captured a bit before them. They were out and about the same time the "Zodiac Killer" was emitting pure-dee havoc throughout the entire Bay Area. However, the Zebras (a name given to them by the media in conjunction with the police because they were four Black men and all of their victims were white) would be charged with and convicted of some 54 or 56 first-degree murders. The exact number evades me today. I used to talk with them on a daily basis. The police kept all of us on a "single cell" status: all five of us were kept in the first five cells as long as we were all together in the hole (Max-B). My rapport with them remains perfect, and hopefully always will.

My discussions, coupled with my travels and learning from the Black Liberation Army, and the tour I had with Uncle Sam's army (we like to say the WRONG army) all proved to make me a very fortunate brother indeed. Living around Huey and Eldridge, along with my big home girl straight out of the hood, Angela Davis, and so many others, allowed me to sponge up some of everything. I would not put such learning into chronological order until prison engulfed me. I exhaled, and took the Temptations' advice from their record titled, *Take a Look Around*.

I always knew that, for some reason, Black folk didn't have things like the whites. Others and myself, when we'd go down East 14th to Montgomery Wards from time to time, even at a tender age, instinct made me aware that an equilibrium was m.i.a. As kids we were happy, I suppose. However, we were also curious and concerned. All kids at some point commence to being inquisitive, and we were no different. Some of the words of the Nation of Islam used at that juncture of my life, I was unable to comprehend the meaning. Yet I had been exposed and absorbed them along with the brothers in the hood, especially big Mark Comfort who arguably is the true founder of the Black Panther Party for Self Defense, and had a very unique vocab. He kept us in his garage telling us about some woodchuck and his birthing something called "lynchings." We heard about brothers being "hung by their balls," and sisters being "impaled." We were told in explicit terms just what the word impaled implied. We had a good ways to go, but the big homies were always at us. It would take some time, but eventually, the seeds commenced to germinate. Some of us were thorns—fuck a rose.

There came a time when we, like everyone else, came to that fork in the road. As can be seen, I veered left. I used to always sit and listen to the brothers and sisters (Elaine Brown and Erika Huggins'nem) chop it up at various spots and locations. We would go up to Grove Street College on the north side right outside of Berkeley. Brothers would be allowed to get on the mic and, as we sometimes called it and sometimes do, "spit!" I'd hear terms being tossed around such as "dialectical materialism," and "lumpen." In hindsight, it was as though I was being prepared to meet, travel, and engage whoever crossed our path when I eventually became annexed to the

BLA. I was not a hindrance, for I knew of terms such as proletarian (they could do no wrong in the eyes of the masses). Mark Comfort would speak about "proletarian morality," being idealistic, and needs to create a more just world. Each event he would go on one, spitting about imperialism and its various forms. He'd spit about us becoming united and harp on such as being a must. All oppressed people must unite against imperialism, he'd say. He lectured the audience on us learning and understanding the concept of becoming anti-imperialist and what they actually meant: "Opposing imperialism means opposing the system where some nations use their power to exploit other nations' wealth." At the time, I understood some, asked questions about that which flew over my head, and some of it didn't really matter at the time.

We knew what the term "nation" implied: a group of people connected by which land being occupied and a common language, economy, and national psychology (mind state). When Huey would come up, he'd sometimes lecture about what is meant by "leftwing" and "rightwing." Left, I'd learn, implies those who tend to judge real world revolutionaries and had no problems using a measuring stick the likes of Jesus, Muhammad, Moses, etc. Ultra-left thus tend to smack of religion which is the first cousin of idealism. A right-winger tends to be conservative, in short. They tend to try to involve tactics as much as duly possible, tend to remain clear of planning and could care less about long term goals. They are primarily made up of people of European descent and tend to be puritanical racists.

I was taught with regard to tactics also. I knew a lil' some-some at an early age, but had nowhere near began to really hone what I had learned up to the point. Tactics are but short term and flexible depending on the situation. Short term plans. Strategy are long term plans to arrive at various goals in route to communism. There must be strategy present at every step of revolutionary struggle. We are to derive confidence from our analysis of the contradictions within imperialism. Entailed, revolutionaries believe it is its own destruction. So, consequently, to concept of internationalism is an absolute must for the oppressed nations if they are to obtain liberation. This type of information was drilled into my head. In time, it would be revisited by me and put to use in a way I deemed it best. For some reason I never liked the word "lumpen" nor used it. To me, it was tantamount to someone "faking the funk" like they were about revolutionary activity, so I never used it. Lumpen nor proletarian. To me, like one of my true OG homies taught me yesteryear, just keep it simple, so I simply say "downtrodden" and be done with it. Sometimes I might just say "poor." Such be the case regarding DOGMATISM. To me, it is simpler to just say "opinion" and be done with it. A dogmatist can be found, generally speaking, without depth, stubborn and very narrow-minded.

Regarding empiricism, I looked deep into the authentic meaning or true definition because it has substance, and I say this because it addressed things one can feel. Empiricism retains the belief that knowledge is derived from experience through direct observation of phenomena. Later, I would encounter Marxists-Leninists, especially while in San Quentin, and we'd have long, beautiful, calm debates. Oftentimes every day, for a while. We would also engage in dialogue on principle contradictions. The principle contradiction comes from dialectical materialism which says that everything can be divided into two opposing forces. These contradictions are the basis for any changes that thing goes through. Defining the principle contradiction is a crucial step to developing ones' political line. The principle contradiction in the world today is between is between the imperialist countries and the countries they exploit. Those in the world today that do not know or can't see this are what Comrade George Jackson referred to as "tombstones." Meaning, in a way, they do not move for anyone or anything, therefore you have to go around them, work around them, or remove them altogether. So, for a time, I studied the pragmatist philosophy, the internationalist philosophy, and ran the entire gauntlet of Marx. This, for many reasons, is why I was really impressed when Huey, Eldridge, or Sister Erika Huggins used to speak. Everybody liked to hear Sister Erika because she used to cuss and it made her seem hella real! From them I learned as they tossed around words such as "line" and their methodology of employing such. Elsewhere I learned how to employ a "soft-line" as well as how to push, politically, a "hard-line." I began following the dictums of Comrade George, in particular his words about "Do only what must be done." I had serious issues with the Marxist-Leninist philosophy, and brother Comrades Mata Musa, Fati Yero, sometimes Mafuholi and Hashima would join us, and we'd go at it. I always retained one of my personal decrees, which was to always deal within the realm of reality. So we talked, exchanged interpretations, and thus, evolved. We retained a pragmatist position, but not that put forth by those whom hail from the West.

So, I retained what was valuable and practical, discarding the rest. No longer a novice, I was a full-fledged soldier of the people and enlisted in the people's army; the Black Liberation Army. I had to fess-up, there were some tenets within the spills of socialism that I embraced, but overall, I was and still today can be found skeptical of theorizing. In short, guessin' will get that ass in tr-r-r-ouble.

My mentor, and by far, my #1 comrade, Imam Muhammad Abdullah of Compton, CA used to tell me, "Allah has a special plan and purpose for you." I have faced death so often, done so much dirt that, if I were to catalogue such, I'd be accused of gross exaggeration for sure. Until my demise or my liberation, I read and write. My weapon of choice, ink and, of course, the mind. No longer the foolish reactionary of times past, with the murders, fights galore, riots, racial disturbances. I have either had to participate in directly or witness first hand. The set-ups and set-backs, with the complete loss of my family, with people I completely trusted and therefore looked up to because I thought they were my close friend, turning on me, even to the extent of doing their doing their very best to have me put on death row and gassed. This done out of fear of me, wanting me off the streets. With the outright witnessing of my celly's murder right before my eyes. With me being woken in the middle of the night by prison guards yelling and screaming at me, "JACKSON! Get him down! Get him down, bend his knees, hold his knees up!" Only to clear my vision and see my celly hanging, straight dead! With prison staff allowing whites to attack and attempt to stab me to death...one would like to think that perhaps I wouldn't have made it this far, if I made it at all, but I'm still here to write about it.

Was it Socrates who said, "Illusions are flawless?" I have heard, seen, and witnessed as much. As I reflect back to when I was at Folsom and the young Crip hung himself as I slept, that very same day, we had played chess. I recall how some things he asked me during the game which didn't seem that out of the ordinary, except this one question. The brother asked me out of the blue, "Aye man, why you come to prison then become a Muslim, change your name and shit?" I told him, "Check this, brother. Listening is important, and a part of communicating is listening, something I've NEVER been good at. We Blacks, collectively, have been religiously brainwashed, and the truth is, no two days are alike. It would take prison to shake me and wake me." He cut me off and told me right to my face,

"Man, ain't no dam God." And that I was full of shit. I had to marshal all of my control and even went so far as to make an excuse to not put hands on him. I never once at that juncture stopped to think that this was his way of seeking help...hard questions. I missed it. I didn't catch it at that time. Only in hindsight. Perhaps I could've save lil' brah's life? The Black race here in North AmeriKKKa have a very complex situation unlike no other people in the recorded history of this planet. And, although we share a common history since being brought here forcefully (with absolutely no choice in the matter), we don't yet understand where each other is coming from far more often than not. This has no root in intellectual sluggishness. No! If I'm ever allowed to tell it, I simply quote the prophet of Islam, Muhammad (pbuh), "Know! What has passed you by was not going to befall you. And what has befallen you was not going to pass you by. The pen has been lifted and the ink has dried." My celly, young Hurk, hung himself that very night. Stiff-necked—literally!

As I reflect now, question have surfaced and must receive an answer. These questions should be on the lips of every Black person here in North AmeriKKKa, if no one else. When I arrived at a full and 100% understanding of the teachings of a person by the name of Elijah Muhammad, he claimed he was taught by God, face to face, for three and a half years flat, non-stop. Please dear reader, go back and re-read that. This shall prove to be of such importance that you cannot afford to miss it this time around. Elijah Muhammad told us (his audience and followers) time and time again, that "We are God's chosen elect!" Read his book, "Message to the Black Man in America" to fully understand what this man taught. You need to obtain an understanding of the remaining schools of thought in Islam. Sunnis follow the lifestyle of Muhammad the Prophet (pbuh), from 1400 years ago; a man who is reported to have never lied. Al-Sunni, in Arabic, actually means "the example." The attachment of the term ul- or "of" in Arabic, was appended after the demise of Muhammad, not during his life. The Sunnis are deeper numerically than any other Islamic school of thought. Al-Shite or Shia is the next largest. The Shi'ites are very learned, and this because they are very big on being well educated and well informed so as to arrive at making well-informed decisions. Their history attests to these words. I have studied the Shi'ite philosophy with a zeal that is almost unreal. I have also studied the Sunni philosophy, and actually practiced it before embracing the Shi'ite school of thought back in '83.

Elijah Muhammad, on the other hand, born and raised here on this stolen soil, in Georgia, taught something totally different. He taught that the BLACK MAN IS GOD in person. No other person in the history of this planet ever made such a claim. Elijah Muhammad claimed that he was taught by God in person, face to face, and that God's true name is Master Farad Muhammad. He taught us that this Farad appeared unto him in the flesh and "raised him up" (taught him), and taught him well. Elijah Muhammad stated unto all with ears to hear that the Black race brought the white race into being. Specifically, a Black man who was a scientist; one of the 24 scientists who every 25 thousand years come together and manifest a "new God."

Farad Muhamad was born in the Holy City of Mecca and came here to AmeriKKKa strictly for the purpose of finding and educating Elijah Muhammad. In particular, educating him about who we, the Black race here today in these 50 colonies (states) really are. That we are originally from a tribe called El-Shabazz. The oldest people to walk this planet. We—those of us who listened—were taught that the white race was brought into being through a grafting experiment by one of our elders named Yakub (so-called Jacob in English). The white race was brought into being through a scientific experiment with the sole purpose of wreaking havoc on this Earth and enslaving the Black race. The white race would rule this planet for 6,000 years, and after that time came and went, they (the white race) would indeed be removed and we (the Black race) would again rule this planet just as we have in times past.

My point for revisiting this philosophy of the true Nation of Islam (I don't recognize Louis Farrakhan) is to state irrefutably that Farrakhan is NOT teaching the exact same teachings that the most Honorable Elijah Muhammad taught. Not by a long shot. Elijah Muhammad taught that the white race was brought into being to do naught but wickedness. If the Black race is indeed responsible for conducting some type of scientific experiment, then whatever the white race has done, are doing, or will do in the future, we the Black race are responsible. This is so, being we are said to have grafted the white race into being. Remember now, Elijah Muhammad has said time and again that the white race was brought into being for the sole purpose of doing evil. Nothing else. Just brought to work evil. From the deeds of the white race, all that his hands have wrought, we Black folks would have forever the direct experience of good and evil, as we are reported to have only experienced good while in "Heaven" (a peaceful state of existence in what some call Africa today). Elijah Muhammad taught us that it was the white race who started all this junk about some place existing up in the sky, a hell somewhere down in the Earth under foot, and of people coming back from the dead. This junk about people coming back from the dead after they have been embalmed and all of their internal organs physically removed (e.g. heart, liver, spleen, both lungs, etc.), yet are to rise one day in the future. This has no merit as no one in the entire history of this planet can prove conclusively that they know someone that has in fact been embalmed, has somehow come back, and has kicked it with whoever. Masons, Shriners, ministers, and preachers all know these to be completely false teachings and that no one is coming, never came, and never will. Yet they take a sworn oath not to ever tell the truth they learn at their secret meetings. Dear reader, this can be discovered simply by your doing independent research. That age old philosophy fits snug here: "Seek, and thou shall find!"

So, our race needs to be about the business of exacting the truth about this person Elijah Muhammad. He was either a true quack or a true man of God the likes of which no people has seen before or after. The message he came with was strictly for us, the tribe of El-Shabazz, stolen from dear sweet Mother Afrika, which I say again here is not the continent's authentic name, but for the sake of argument and time consumption, I will use it for now.

Aside from Brothers Marcus Garvey and Noble Drew Ali, no other person has stepped to the plate and spoken out with regard to the truth like this man Elijah Muhammad. One may say Malcolm X did, however, look at Malcolm's entire track record. Review it very carefully; meticulously. Read his "Autobiography" very carefully. Malcolm gave a list of Black brother's names to a pig in the city of Chicago. If you or I did that, they would label you or me as a sho'nuff snitch. Why not Malcolm? He talked a good one early on, straight from the gate, but slowly he began to associate with the Nabby Jones KKKamp, and look what he up and did after all he established. Look what it cost him: his home bombed, his wife frightened out of her wits. And Sister Betty was a down sister, a good, solid sister. Rare and of good quality like Sister Winnie Mandela...Nelson, once freed, commenced to take up with Nab'nem too. I make no apology to the family of Malcolm for I believe a person who won't tell it like it is, is a liar. Plain and simple. So, the *64 Million Dollar Question* remains, is the Black man God? Is there any way at all anyone can do that which would disprove conclusively that Elijah Muhammad never actually met and talked with God in person? Are we in fact exactly who he claimed we are or not? With all the religious scholars abroad, with all the Al Sharptons, the Billy Grahams, Rev. K.C. Prices, and so forth, all this knowledge they're supposed to have and are supposed to fear naught but God, how come these above named individuals and many, many others clean smooth around the world haven't and won't step up to prove one way or another just who this Brother Elijah Muhammad actually was? The year our possible savior passed away—1975—wasn't that long ago. I say possible because, for now, I will reserve my position until such time arise that appears to warranted that I shine the light on just exactly what my position is.

I think I would be remiss to not make mention of the righteous Hebrews. The Yahweh philosophy, in particular those in Florida, and of course those over in the Mother Land that yet cling to the teachings of the original script. You true Hebrews—not those who have bit and annexed selves with the "squatters" in Palestine pretending as well as killing the righteous like it's being conducted in the name of their supreme being. They need to stop it, but knowingly, they never will, so the Muslims must take a step back there and rethink their position like never before. No Arafat-type band-aid solutions, you see what that got you all there in Palestine??? And realistically, to think that the counterfeit Israelis are gonna someday "see the light," pack up their things, and leave all that they have built unto you Muslims, Palestinians, Lebanese, etc. Knock it off. Best hurry up and re-enter the realm of reality because, sure as shit stank, those would-be Jews ain't going no dam where. So you either going to have to devise a new strategy or come up with something new altogether, unless you are going to finally go on and recognize Israel's right to exist.

Sunni and Shi'ites. Man o' man. I was born right here in North AmeriKKKa yet have come across the root of the two of yours problem. I have read about the matter concerning Muhammad's (pbuh) decree unto Ali upon his demise and what was said at Ghardir Khum. I tell any of you the following, and I only wish I could speak with any Sheik, Imam, or Ayatollah, I would tell them thus: Seriously, you mean to tell me that you are yet in 2011 and still fighting over the Ghardir Khum incident? You mean to tell me, that after all the ikhwanul muslimeen (Muslim brotherhood) has been through, the many wars fought over the continent of Asia, and deep into the interior of Africa and further abroad, in Indonesia, and on and on, that you still don't recognize who it is that keeps this religious issue going? Iran, you talk all the "great Satan" bullshit, yet apparently don't know of or so much as adhere to the dictums of Mr. Sun Tzu. You don't know the art of war, Iran? I know that Germany invaded your land twice and renamed it Iran (Land of the Aryans)...why don't you spend your time and money getting back at them? Check them? You spend time, money, and hella energy tripping on your next door neighbor, Iraq, but are never heard to say so much as a word about what the Germ-man and Germ-people have done to you.

Unto any Sunni anywhere on this funky-ass planet, you harp so much about all the hadiths that were written and your interpretation is so pristine, and all of you "Bin Laden boys" running around moving on folks all over the planet—why don't you get your house in order? And, should anyone wonder what Ashanti means by that, get your own house in order. Shi-i-i-it, be glad to tell ya. The Sunnis claim that Ali ibn Talib, a brother who would grow up to marry the Prophet's daughter, Lady Fatima, would become the father of two offspring, Hasan and Husain. Ali ibn Talib (he was the son of a brother named Talib) was considered the founder of what many today call Shi'ite or Shia Muslims. Shi'ite or Shia means "those who follow the household of the Holy Prophet, Muhammad." Nothing more, nothing less. Muhammad is said to have made a stop as he returned from Hajj (pilgrimage) at a place called Ghardir Khum. Arguably, this area today is called Medina. In any event, Muhammad (pbuh) is reported to have given a khutbah (sermon or lecture) there and during such, he uttered the words, "Upon my demise, Ali is best qualified to lead my Umma/ Nation, and I therefore elect him to act in my stead." Those present, from that point on referred to themselves as Shi'ites (those who follow the household of the Holy Prophet, Muhammad) and Ali, married to the Prophet's daughter, was as "household" as household could get.

On the flip side of the coin, the Sunnis claimed that they were not present and, because of such, they deem the claim as baseless and lacking authenticity, and refused to honor such a claim. The Sunnis began to actually persecute the Shi'ites. Many of them were buried alive inside walls in a vertical/ standing position. This "many" of which I speak include some of the Prophet's own family members. Immediate family members at that.

Do your research... The Shi'ites would be hunted down like unto the witch hunts carried out in Salem, Massachusetts and such.

The Shi'ites would be forced to go underground. The Sunnis continued to grow numerically. In the interim, Muslims have engaged in numerous wars, some that have not stopped to this very day. They have fought wars against tyranny, they have fought wars due to rank leaders in various countries. Muslims had fought wars against oppression, wars against their rights being suppressed, and wars against invading forces—namely Roman Catholicism. They were the Robin Hoods of the day. We must, dear reader, come to an understanding of just exactly what brought on all this bloodletting all over the world, because surely, and I hate to say this, but the Muslims have indeed succeeded in turning the entire world against them like never before. Even the hatred of Muslims during the Crusades miserably pales in comparison to the sheer number of people who hate Muslims today. Muslims are truly the scum of the Earth in the eyes of not many, but most. A fact! A lot of this thanks to Osama bin Laden, although personally, I have reason to believe he was just a scapegoat. Like always, the gullible masses bit, hook, line, and sinker, and will continue to do so until they get a thorough knowledge that the "Illuminati" not only exists, but are fine and dandy. Better believe it. Their power is just unbelievable. This is where their strength lay, in the people's consistent disbelief that such massive conspiracies exist. So, they blueprint deeds to be carried out, and have been successful for centuries on end. Repeatedly, our forefathers left us clear instructions of who and what to be on the lookout for. In contemporary times, none have warned us so more sternly than Noble Drew Ali, Marcus Garvey, and Elijah Muhammad.

History has inscrolled that the devil-folk have not missed an opportunity to exploit us and turn us one against the other. Such has been conducted mainly through infiltration. In fact, it can be said that the only entity that team Lucifer has not outright infiltrated is the mighty Moorish Science Temple here in the united snakes. Recently I was approached by some individuals deeply involved in the occupying scene in the Bay Area. I said that to say this: I told them to forever be mindful of both Sisters Tubman and Sojourner Truth, and to keep uppermost in mind the fate of Brothers Denmark Vessey, Gabriel Prosser, Nat Turner, and any and all other movements. They all had the same outcome: they were infiltrated and divided. Name it, and the devilish folks can claim it. I told the youngsters to be forever on the lookout for those advocating violence. They will appear and disappear. Appear, and disappear. Appear, and disappear. This is an undercover pig—the disappearance is them checking-in/reporting.

Allow me to say, at least the bulk of Sunni and Shi'ite are good people. Natural born soldiers. This history of the Muslim or Moslem ranging from Mecca to their Spanish conquest clearly display a folk who don't accept wooden nickels. Far more deadly than even the Japanese kamikaze they are. No people ever to walked this earth has displayed such clear-cut fierce loyalty as have the Muslim. Their dedication to that which they profess and partisan has no rival in all of history.

I sallied forth an avalanche of information for the youngsters and composed it where even the layman could comprehend it. I took them, painstaking as it was, all the back way to the so-called Big-Bang Theory and "triple darkness" philosophy. I explained to them what is meant by and who Yakub is in terms of history, what history says with regard to the 24 scientists and the genetic experiment they under took and completed, creating what some refer to as "Caucasoid." Most of the exchange of info took place while I was at Jamestown State Prison. It took me just a bit over two years to bring them up to speed, so to speak. We debated for some 14 months whether it was possible for a people to have at one time populated this planet with all of their brain cells fully functioning. A subject I love without reservation. Such actually explained how our people built the great pyramids and performed other deeds which today's world refers to as "miracles!" I explained it was Mr. Yacub (Jacob in so-called English) was the head of the 24 scientists and he left ultra-ultra-ultra instructions for his flock to carry out, and they did. They removed "genes" from folks and introduced such onto another human reportedly until such time they produced what some today call white! As we ourselves have come to witness today, the question of DNA is hotter than lava. All the more when one considers that the so-called first "DNA convictions" jumped in 1987. This speaks volumes.

I know well of and about the so-called First Amendment and freedom of speech. Arguably, a good thing. But, how about this: We have heard plainly time and again about Adolf Hitler and the indifferent, precarious, and rambunctious situation he brought into being. It has received a fixed place in history. Not the same with regards to the teachings of the Nation of Islam. Everybody tends to stay clear, and I do not believe that each and every persons does so out of fear they will get "hit" by the NOI. No! To the contrary, most people, especially young brothers (and I know this to be true because I have taken polls myself for more than a decade) wherever I go, they just don't know about what this man Elijah Muhammad taught. They know even less still when Hitler's name is mentioned. Most young brothers (except KRS-One, Paris, Canibus and a few others) only know that Hitler hated us niggas, that's it and that's all. They cannot go even a little deeper in conversation with you about Hitler or Elijah Muhammad. "Oh, you mean dem Muslims? Yea, my pops fucked wittum for ah minut', man," is normally the response you get from a brothers in his 20s or 30s, and a hell of a lot of them in their 40s. If you ask a young brother about Hitler's Germany, just what is a "Nazi," the young brother will be lost for words. If you ask young brothers if they like the TVs show "Jeopardy," man, they almost pitch a fit. "Hell naw, man. I ain't into that ole' shit shanwtay," they'll say. Again, my throat stay parched from talking to the youngsters, trying to make them understand what they need to understand. I initiated classes here as the opportunity availed itself. Brothers don't know, and don't care to know. Yet, *aluta continua*, the struggle continues.

People protest and are up in arms about all sorts of events, misdeeds, and erroneous claims, some major, some minor. Howzabout we come together and petition for release of the Nation of Islam files held by the FBI, as compiled by J. Edgar Hoover? Naw, on second thought, why don't we ourselves do our own personal research and present it to the world? If we are found partisan of what Elijah Muhammad taught, we henceforth proclaim unto the entire world, "Ay yo! Yo! Listen up! We Black Folk really are the Gods of the Universe. You heard me correct: We Blacks are God! Look in your Bible yourself. Psalms 82:6." Force preachers and such peers to explain just exactly what that verse is in regards to, because someone in the Bible is telling somebody that "Ye are Gods."

If we conclude, once and for all, that Elijah Muhammad's message was a lie, one giant hoax, then the Nation of Islam should be put on trial for war crimes. Yes, WAR CRIMES! For destroying a people's minds, just as we have claimed the white man did to us during slavery (and the white man did indeed), then the Nation of Islam should be brought to trial. America, do you not run a TV commercial to this very day stating, "A mind is a terrible thing to waste?" Well, let's not play around any further.

Who has the balls to delve into this most serious of serious questions and present their findings to the world? True, Germans "physically" assaulted the Jews. If the teachings of Master Fard Muhammad as taught by Elijah Muhammad should ever prove purposefully wrong, purposefully made up, and the Nation of Islam is still teaching the same, will the self-proclaimed, self-righteous AmeriKKKan government not stop it and , as they say, do the right thing? Not merely put a stop to it, but bring charges up on those responsible for the destruction of the minds of many. Perhaps as many as four million! This is a form of war if—and I reiterate IF—the teaching are ever found to be a hoax. Was it not Elijah Muhammad who used to have printed in his "Muhammad Speaks" newspaper that he would give money out of the vest pocket of one of his brothers if you or anyone else on Earth can prove just one word of his teachings to be false. Just one word. Not a paragraph, not even a sentence. Just one single, solitary word. I used to read those words all the time in the Muhammad Speaks newspaper. Surely Nab Jones'nem, with all the technology and informants and information from all around the entire globe, can track down one of the old, original newspaper of the Nation of Islam? What's the matter AmeriKKKan government?

What's the matter Pat Robertson and the 700 Club? What's the matter Jerry Fallwell, and your so-called moral majority? What's the matter Rev. K.C. Price out there in L.A., and Pastor John Hagee? What's the matter all you popes and rabbis? What's the matter? Cat got your tongue? I believe the amount of money offered up by Elijah Muhammad was 50-grand for any human being who could prove just one word of his teachings to be wrong. Not a peep from none of the above and not a word from all the other hating ass would-be co-called ministers. Jesse Jackson, what say you? Aye, Al Sharpton, yeah, I'm talking to you…what say you on this question of absolute, utmost importance? Aye, New Republic of Africa, thought y'all loved your kith and kin and were desirous of seeing them truly free. What say you on this question? Aye, New Black Panthers, what say you? Yo! Billy Gates, you got paper up tha ass, surely you can fund an investigation into this question. Where's all your benevolence and Good Samaritan endeavors at now? Aye, Hearst, you have so much paper you wipe ya ass with 50s and 100s. What say you? Team up with Billy Gates and foot the bill—show the entire world you are really and truly good people. Aye, Spike Lee, you talk about that, "Do the Right Thing" shit, well, do the right thing here, "brother." Getting kinda hot under the collar now, huh y'all? Masonic orders and Shriner's secret society lodges around the globe, if nobody else has power and wherewithal, you do. Why don't you step up to the plate? I'm just wondering, could it be true you *already* know the real but won't come clean? That's the word on the streets regarding you, anyway.

Let it be known, one way or another, sooner or later, hook or crook, the truth and secrets have a way of freeing themselves over time. Think it may just be the Muslims (the 5%) know the real. They are far removed from being hoodwinked, and you cowards listed know it and stay clear so as to not make waves and arouse the youth of this CORPORATE EMPIRE. Newsflash: They are gonna learn and discern anyway. With or without your endorsement, and despite your best efforts to hide the real in symbolic fashion. You will kill me, of this I am certain, but there shall be many-many-many more "me's." Believe that.

Now, back to the dam question. Which one of you trifflin'ass, fake ass ministers, capitalists, and secret society members gonna stand up and accept my challenge? Yea, that's what I thought. It's gonna be hella hard to get this book published in of itself, let alone get this message out, but I have something in place for my untimely demise, and the spotlight will remain pointed on those lyin' ass, fake ass individuals who know the truth, yet hide it. To top it off, got nerve to get mad at me and label me as a militant and psychopathic serial killer and the like. No! What you need to do is listen to my Brother Michael Jackson's cut, "Man in the Mirror." Yeah, try that on for size. All of you need to hear this, need to be told this, need to be confronted, straight jammed, and that's what this is about. Jammin' ya ass, pulling ya ho'card. Why do you try getting your Carol O'Conner/Archie Bunker on, and call a spade a spade? You fuckin' cowards. I have no respect for any of you, and just for the record, the time has surfaced for me to state my position regarding the teachings of the Most Honorable Elijah Muhammad. He was 100% correct, every word of it. Moreover, Farrakhan, you need to stop playing, brah, and return to the fold. Start spittin' the real you know your people so very badly need to hear like never before. I understand you have been under the weather. If true, appoint your offspring with stern instructions, as well as your brother-ministers in temples across this corporate empire. Tell them to go all out with getting the truth out there. You know I am right, brother. I had your tape in Quentin, Brother Farrakhan, titled *It's a Nigger in the Yard*. Perhaps your best work. You spoke about Whoopi Goldberg and her Jewish name, that you know "somebody making whoopee," and so on. I've told brothers everywhere I go about that cassette tape you made in what, '79? '79? Or whatever it was, I had it. And that's when you were Farrakhan, and your tongue was truly on fire. Not anymore. Too much drinking ice water, brother. You been sipping on way too many water coolers my man. Remember back to when you call the Jewish religion a "gutter religion" and all the flack you received? Peeped you on Arsenio Hall yesteryear. You stood tall through it all. Old gray mule just ain't what it used to be. If the moccasin fit, get ya dam foot in t. You know da bidness!!

Won't nobody stand up and challenge whether or not the teaching of the honorable Elijah Muhammad was the truth or not. Won't no Imam, Nation of Islam Minister reeeealy put it out there in its original format. I ain't got no love or respect for none of y'all. Quiet as a cemetery. Make me wanna call you something, but the deen (religion) instructs us to be humble. It's hard, however, to remain humble when surrounded by all these good faking the funk ass—gotta lot of nerve, yet you supposed to be down for your people. Only good from the safety of the pulpit. Get the fuck outta here. Ministers, alright. Cowards in the first degree.

Some of us, we heard the teachings by the Lamb, took them to heart, then went out and acted on them, right or wrong. Point being, look what it cost us. Look at what we have sacrificed. Look at Brother Talmage Hare 'nem. Actually look. Them Jersey brothers couldn't hack what Malcolm was saying about the Lamb. Look at the so-called Zebra Killers, here in prison with me! I mean, comon' man. How much more serious could a brother or brothers be? Then too, why hasn't anyone stood up—the TV show 60 Minutes, 20/20, whoever man, who the fuck ever, and ask the question? If Elijah Muhammad "fathered" all these children, where the hell are they now? We have DNA in the house now, Jack! Where are these offspring? How come 60 Minutes hasn't sought them out to have on their show like they do every dam body else? "Tick, tick, tick, tick, tick, Hi! I'm Mike Wallace. I'm Leslie Stahl, I'm whothefuckever, and this is another edition of 60 Minutes. Tonight, the long lost forgotten children of the man who called himself the Lamb of God, Elijah Muhammad. Now such-and-such age, here is so-and-so." That would raise your ratings clean smooth through the dam sky itself.

Hey Geraldo, where the hell your good hoopla, good story-seeking ass at? How come you haven't stepped to the plate? Pecks running round here sweating Brother Barry Bonds and shit, spotlighting the likes of Jose Canseco and the masses. Thought you United Negro ass tricks was about that Mind-is-a-Terrible Thing-to-Waste-ism. Thought this government was about doing right? Thought you didn't step on freedom of religion's toes but that would just be damed if you didn't stand idly by while a person get his Hitler on, minus the gas chamber. Y'all full of shit. Everybody I've named herein is full of shit. Got the nerve to be rippin' and runnin' all around the globe straight killing folks. Gaddafi and his children too. Y'all AmeriKKKan government killed not just Gaddafi, but murdered his children too. Yep! Did Saddam Hussein and his children—took them out. Put them in place and when they decided to do for self and say fuck y'all, you smoked them. What book publisher is gonna have the nut-sack hanging to publish this? Comrade George Lester Jackson was more than 100% correct when he wrote about "Everywhere the white man's foot has tread, he left a trail of blood. You cannot go anywhere the white man has been and not find theft of land, raping of women, killing of men, plundering of their natural resources, and a firm denial thereof." Stupid ass people can't even see this, yet jumping toady. Dumb ass. That's why I love folks like that rap group Dead Prez! Hell yeah, how can I not? How can you would-be lukewarm ass so-called revolutionaries not likw Dead Prez, in particular their first release, "Let's Get Free?" A nuclear bomb indeed, I salute you Dead Prez. Whattup, M-1? Love y'all man. Stay down. You got ya head on correct and don't you ever allow anyone to tell you otherwise. Y'all know the bidness!!!

I would like to stop, exhale so to speak, and spit a 'lil some-some about them so-called Zionists. Being that they have ripped the heart out of the media world-wide, most brothers don't really know what Zionism is, let alone its authentic history. Like the lead rapper of the X-Clan, Brother Grand Verbalizer said, "Why is that?" You would be Jews have done unto the Muslims what you claim Hitler did unto you. Good for the geese, good for the gander-ism. Chicken, brang dat ass on home so you can roost. UN partition plan. Pecks taking folks land. Kidnappers in the first degree. Squatters, especially in Palestine and South Africa. Lotta nerves, boy I tell you. Remember Comrade George's words: Peep the 'woods food print trail, y'all, peep it. Follow it y'all, don't lose sight, after all, you are from Africa, you can dam'sho track shit. Follow their bloody footprint trail. See what I mean? See what Comrade George meant? Dirt. And in the hundreds of millions if you count collectively all the Asians (Japanese), all the Africans (slavery), all the Indians (both India and North American), stole land from the Mexicans, beat the Eskimos out of Alaska...paid what for Alaska, $20 mil?? Daammn, the Eskimos were making $20 million a year off of sardines alone. A mammoth beat move. To quote Brother Ice Cube, "Do the math."

Zionism actually started in the 1800s in Europe. Their goal was to establish a homeland, so they say. The so-called Jews get more than a trillion dollars out of the Red Sea each year alone, so that could be why they really wanted the land. They set their sights on Palestine. They filtered into Palestine, and before you knew it, they were there in NUMBERS. So much so that fighting broke out. Got hella ugly, fast. The United Nations boys stepped in with compound words such as, "self-determination" and the like. A war would erupt in 1947 and last into 1949. It was a grizzly war for the Muslims/ Palestinians. Zionists showed Muslims no mercy. It was reported in Islamic papers that the Zionists committed at least 16 massacres, killing men, women, and children repeatedly and in the 100s per whop! To quote Brother Will Smith, "molly-wopped" was the word. The Zionists dug the Muslims clean, smooth out. Went on a building spree, and from the building spree, they went on a spreading spree. Took more and more Arab land. Then they took even more land still. They disarmed the Arabs much like you can still see today. The Arabs only have rocks to throw at the squatters. Palestinians got their hat brought to them, or perhaps I should say their turbans. All's quiet on the western front, so to speak. The Arabs would dare to step to the Hebrews are brothers and there would be birthed what some call "The Six Day War." If you think the first molly-whop was bad, you ain't heard nothing, to quote Stevie Wonder. The counterfeit, impoverished-ish, gutter religion-ass Jews really took it to them this time. The Muslims, Arabs, or whatever title you care to dress them in, they got their ass tore up from the floor up. Or, from the desert to their cities. Them Jews was on that ass. Didn't take but six days to down the Arabs. Six days. Israel had conquered some 80% of Palestine.

In 1967 the artificial, 100% fake wanna-be Jews had mobbed the Palestinians out of even more still. Foul be the word! What's jumping in this very country right now, the "occupation" of various colleges/ universities, turf, of sort, in Oakland and other spots was hella old. Ask a Jew. That's all you got to do, ask any Jew what he or she knows about the word occupy, then brace ya self. Fake-ass Jews once occupied part of Egypt, but later unassed it. Did the same with Syria, and it is occupied up to present day. Dam shame. We know about Jay-Z and Beyoncé, all about the Super Bowls, and who won what at the music awards. Know all about Pac and Big (both r.i.p.), know all about Motown and who did what, can sing entire James Brown and Temptations albums by heart. Not a .45, hell naw, an entire LP! We know statistics galore about trivial shit, yet know little to nothing about why the Muslims hate AmeriKKKa and the Jews, wherever they be found.

Why brothers and sisters be getting in the squatters' ass in South Africa? Fucking them off every chance they get? Why not? They dam'sho did it to the brothers and sisters. 'Woods have killed entire tribes off in Africa. Whole, entire tribes. I can actually list about 18 straight off the top of my head, Johnny-on-the-spot. You can get up on such simply by getting the book *Outline of History*, volumes one and two, by H.G. Welles. And be sure to get a copy of Brother J.A. Rogers work titled, *From Superman to Man*, and *World's Great Men of Color*, volumes one and two. And his work *Sex and Race*, volumes one and two. Serious bombs. Also check out these books for a proper understanding of Islam: *Najul Balagha* by Imam Ali. It is the best book ever written, bar none—in my opinion. He outdid everyone from every era. Get *Brother of the Prophet Muhammad, Imam Ali*, volumes one and two. And be sure to get a copy of the absolutely pertinent, *Husain, The Savior of Islam*. A must read.

In 1948, Israel mobbed the Palestinians out of the last 22% of their land/ the West Bank and Gaza Strip. Oh, it was on fa'sho now if it was never on before. The squatterism, fake-ass Jews were so violent-prone, they even attacked a U.S. Navy ship (the U.S. Liberty) killing and injuring more than 200 Americans. Lydon B. Johnson let it slide. I mean, after all, he and his clandestine crew had just smoked Kennedy, so they didn't need any more heat in the kitchen. That would come up later. Once again, Jews got away with mass murder and there wasn't so much as a peep from the American public. Haveth thou eyes and seeith not? Haveth thou ears and heareth not? I guess not. But, at that time, let a Panther so much as lay a baby finger on a pig. Remember, this was '67. So much shit was in effect. Southeast Asia was on a poppin. France had their hat brought to them and so entered big brother. Inside these very states, shit was on in the worst way. The Watts Riot had just simmered, and Black folk had started to question MLKs philosophy of non-violence 'cause too many of us were getting dug out. Stokely and SNCC were like, maybe them Panthers are on to something. Fred Hampton and Crew, Bunchy and crew, George, Huey, Eldridge and crew as well as those up in Washington state. All putting in some work at various levels. Out of Vietnam was the word. Soon, words entailing a demand to divest or else started to spread. Get out of South Africa. Here in the U.S.A., so much was jumping it was hard to keep track, all the more so for those of us in our teens or early 20s. But we were on point. An alarm had been sounded informing us: The devil has tip-toed into heaven while God slept.

As God began to stir, things began to happen. As he was an angry God, a real-real angry God. A God that is uninterested in explanations. Word had it, he uttered, "Vengeance is mine!" So we peep game as God prepared to do this thang. It was now time to shank n' fingerpop!!
          "I have said, ye are gods."
                Proverbs 82:6

The Honorable Elijah Muhammad came with a message to help all Black folk here in the wilderness of North AmeriKKKa. Why we say "wilderness" is simply because this place is full of wild beasts. His message was to inspire all who had ears to hear to seriously, like never before, step up to the plate, and try with your absolute all to totally knock out negative behavior—robbery, murder, oppression, stealing, drinking, fornicating, and so on.

During my time at Folsom State Prison, I had started construction of a "jamat" (Arabic for "group"). It would not really blossom and become an absolute force until we all were finally let out of the hole. "We" including in Brother-comrade Mujahid Abdullah. This brother is one of the most gifted thinkers I've come across in all my years in prison. He is truly a gifted thinker. I gave him the name Mujahid because I saw in him a brother who was righteous and strived for justice and fair play. He would no longer adhere to the street gang name of Cry Baby Sal! He, along with Brothers Ramzadin and Malik—both surnamed Abdullah. They would help in organizing, but nowhere near like Brother-comrade Mujahid. It would be he and I who would become cellies, and during this time we would study in a manner the likes of which probably has no peer. This was conducted daily and without fail. We studied everything of interest. We delved into all walks and manners of life and philosophy that had a significant effect on the masses at some juncture in recorded history. Indeed, we conducted a clandestine perfunctory investigation into all gangs and religious entities, and not only in Folsom. We investigated those in free society as well.

One of our major concerns were the teachings of one W.D. Muhammad, son of the Honorable Elijah Muhammad, and what he was doing in terms of leadership of his father's flock. We did not endorse what he was doing nor the direction had he been leading his followers for more than a decade. We engaged in comparative research, too. We compared books of a sort to other books addressing the same subject matter. We gave a very close look at past and present leaders and what caused their demise. In some cases, such as that of Marcus Garvey, we studied what brought them a measure of success before Nab Jones and company brought him down on counterfeit charges.

In time, Brother Mujahid and I would go so far as to establish a line of communication with brothers across this country. Some, I knew from my days of traveling with the Black Liberation Army. Others, I had established contact with, such as Larry Hoover's Vice Lords, the Hebrew partisans of Yahweh ben Yahweh in Florida, the Latin Kings, the El-Rukins, the Black Gangster Disciples—of which I have a cousin on my father's side who is a member in Chi-town and the well-organized Ummah Nation in Brooklyn where I have peeps on my mom's side. We established contact and maintained it with the earmarks of true soldiers at work.

We organized from within, and gradually attracted many from without. Together, Brother Mujahid and I composed a constitution and it was sent across AmeriKKKa to both Sunni and Shi'ite Muslims whom we had previous contact with. This constitution was endorsed in Baltimore, Philly, New Jersey, Brooklyn, Chicago, Ohio, Texas, Los Angeles, and some 12 other cities. Mujahid came up with the concept of "A.L.I.," which is actually symbolic for the Islamic Liberation Army spelled backwards: A.L.I. / I.L.A. It caught on. By 1987, we were stronger than the underarm of King Kong. Various former concerns were rehashed. Of them, some of the majors were what is and should be our position with regard to W.D. Muhammad. He was of major concern, especially to the Sunni faction amongst us. Sister Angela Davis was another concern as she is believed by some to have sold out and gave information to the FBI with regard to Comrade George Jackson's alleged escape attempt back in '71. Then there was Louis

Farrakhan. He knows not, but he'd be dead right now if not for the Shi'ite Muslims at Folsom and one Sunni in Los Angeles.

We, the Muslim Brotherhood and the A.L.I. / I.L.A., conversed with the Bloods and Crips, and got them to approve a peace treaty initiative. We then had Hall of Fame football player Jim Brown contacted and asked to host the endeavor, being that he is known by Crips and Bloods in Los Angeles. He agreed to host it at his estate. Now, I.L.A. took great strides to sway Minister Louis Farrakhan to fly out to Los Angeles and engage the peace treaty attempt to be held at Jim Brown's house. It took some doing, but Farrakhan signed on...not knowing that in fact he had agreed to fly out to California and be duly assassinated at the meeting. It is worth mentioning once again that specific Sunnis really wanted Farrakhan done away with. When it came time for us to cast our vote, three 'rades strongly disagreed, rationalizing the "what if" card, meaning "what if" some Crips or Bloods decide to go down with Farrakhan. Then what? Moreover, it was a given that Farrakhan would have along with him members of their military arm, the Fruit of Islam (FOI), for security.

The three brothers at Folsom concerned themselves with such and advanced that they would not—and simply could not—be part of such an undertaking. They knew that if we knocked Farrakhan down, we'd have to eradicate more "brothers" than just him. The Folsom A.L.I.s voted a firm NO. Then, a major Sunni out in L.A. joined us. An Uzi machine gun would have been pulled on Farrakhan in a garage also. Not one, but two imams would be found dead, killed in other states, alongside the freeway. Then the Shi'ite became irate. They additionally wanted to "hit" a brother group or entity known as the Jamaican Posse, claiming that the JPs were contaminating the various neighborhoods by selling dope. Their plan was that the I.L.A. could use the monies gained in the lick to purchase more land, weapons, vans, and the like. Enter the Sunnis. They would not hear of it and promptly took steps to shut this idea down before it could begin to grow. It may also be noteworthy that the FBI became aware of our existence and they knew some of our plans. Certainly the one concerning Mr. Louis Farrakhan, as they paid me a visit and asked me an avalanche of questions. They were also concerned about the two imams found slain in New York and Ohio. Still, somehow we managed to keep things under wraps and didn't let them get out of control. However, because of some of the aforementioned topics, some of the brotherhood no longer dialogued with others. Bad blood. We had an incident of major proportion when Imam Muhammad Abdullah was on the Los Angeles Freeway and had a car pull up next to him. The individual riding shotgun pulled an Uzi on him, but didn't fire. We knew it to be specific Shi'ites. These same ones pulled an Uzi on him in a garage behind his voting against the move on the Jamaican Posse. I made recommendations, they were accepted, and we were on chill mode. Contemplation was in order.

As history attests, it would come to pass that A.L.I. never once took a brother out, and we most certainly did not approve of the double murders in New York and Ohio. Both were done out of our jurisdiction. So consequentially, Farrakhan, Sister Angela Davis, and the Jamaican Posse were all by-passed. I did not birth an entity into being merely to move on my own. We had a written code of ethics, too, Brother Mujahid and I. We both knew what we were doing and what we wanted, and in no way, shape, or form incognizant of what we had brought into existence. What we wanted was LAND. To generate our own foods while simultaneously and constantly reaching out to foreign countries for various forms of aid. Nothing to do with taking out our own. In fact, that was one of the concerns we were dead set against.

Today, as I compose this, Minister Louis Farrakhan is alive, Sister Angela Davis is alive, and not one Jamaican Posse member has ever been assaulted by us. And, might I add, A.L.I. / I.L.A. is still alive and vibrant. Maturation via time has taught us much. Among that taught, the philosophy of two wrongs don't make a right.

We live on, we live right, and we refuse otherwise. I.L.A. all the way. Soldier-in, soldier-out. Of that let there be no doubt! I recall vividly how my mother used to say I wouldn't make it into my 20s. Well, I'm in my 60s now. I have come to witness quite a bit, to the extent some have repeatedly asked me to capture my views and experience on paper. This you now are reading is annex to just such a request.

Right here and now in my 60s, I cannot put a finger on exactly what it was that made me such a fan and student of history. Folks tell me the story of when my mother went into labor. Her water broke and she was rushed out of the house, down the stairs, and en route, the neighbor's big, super-aggressive German shepherd was between my mother, the partisans, and the car. Rex, Eddie and Paul Jones' dog, had somehow liberated itself from their backyard, attacked my mother, and bit her something vicious. Folks claim it had a werewolf effect on me because of the way I turned out. Hmmm...

In my philosophy course I'd learn all thoughts are on a frequency and always return to their source. The philosophy of the Eastern Stars female covert entity teaches what one attracts is in direct accord with what they think. It is called magnetic energy in the science world. Follow me now...Every thought is in fact and in truth a creation. All thoughts create. Because my race is so confused and confounded, they yet not understand what the philosophy of "made in the image of God" really implies. It only gets worse when you try to explain to them why some say and believe that the Black man is God! I concerned self with the philosophy of who's the bigger fool: the fool, or the fool who follows the fool? I'm going to make an attempt to contrast this here and now.

I have every reason to believe that a sound mind neither advances the notion of counterfeit, nor is it to be found making any attempt to integrate a correct line of thought with artificiality, knowing that, to do so, the end results would be imbalance. I knew years ago that parents are not supposed to out-live their children. I was taught and see the real. I was made aware of, believe, and advance the teachings that the miseducation of my kith started with slavery. I, myself, have witnessed generations lost. WWI, WWII, the Korean War, an entire generation lost to the Vietnam War. I've witnessed first-hand a generation and a half lost all due to the so-called drug wars. It gets worse if I tally up the lives of my own gone and forgotten due to the Blood and Crip war. I knew, in all of this blood-letting, there was a message. I knew it. It only stands to reason that there would be. So I set out to see if I could decipher it. Sounds like I'm rambling, don't it? No, I'm not; I'm leading the reader to a place we'll arrive at in a bit. All things must have a foundation.

If memory serves correct, it was Brother Martin Luther King, Jr. who once said, "A moral man or woman has the right to violate unjust laws." Since my birth and reaching an age of understanding words, information has come my way. I can remember clear as a church house bell on Sunday morning the first time I heard brothers talking about a sister, the only female in history who became a pharaoh. I dam near fell down. My father and Brother Mark Comfort talking 'round the dinner table about Black Wall Street and how the white man destroyed it. Black Wall Street was located in the state of Oklahoma. By their lonesome, Blacks there built a bus system, some 21 churches, two restaurants, more than 30 grocery stores, and at least 600 successful businesses. All outright destroyed. A Black built, owned, and operated hospital, bank, post office, three schools, a law firm, a library, 17 privately owned air planes, a movie theatre—all this destroyed, notwithstanding some 3,000 Blacks dead and untold numbers seriously injured. I asked myself, how could this be? I'm uncertain, but I've been made privy that Blacks sold B.E.T., yet I'm hearing absolutely nothing about mine endeavoring to emulate Tulsa, Oklahoma. Nothing has reached me with regard to mine purchasing radio transmitters, television and radio broadcasts and stations, nor us brothers rising to challenge what some refer to as the dominant language. We have here of late done a lil' some-some in terms of engendering publishing companies. But we truly have a ways to go and a hard row to hoe!

I used to trip on how my father always talked about "cracker this" and "cracker that." His words about how there is always a whiteboy running around the planet, sympathetic, who knows what's best for us and is gonna save us. This been jumping long before cracker Jim Jones and his crew in so-called Jonestown, Guyana had sisters instructing their offspring to listen to this nut and drink poison. Over 900 Black folks followed this dude. Pops knew thangs. Me, I was learning them. In time, I'd put that horse and carriage together.

It would become clear to me why in the USA people take to the streets in protest and riot. They are doing so this very day with regard to lil' brah Trayvon Martin's case. And like they did regarding the beating of Brother Rodney King—peep it closely. There is the overturning of cars, smashing windows, arson, and so forth, but we do nothing over our children being molested. We say zero over straight, proven corruption. Our youth killing youth, and I shall spare the reader of those amongst us who have dared to join—get this now—Roman Catholicism and them so-called "fathers" plain wrecking shop with our young. Rape be the word. Ask the question, dear reader: Just how much money has the Catholic Church paid out to hush-up folks who have filed paperwork on them for sexual abuse? I concluded a re-examination of the role played by the white race since the beginning of recorded history was in order—especially European expansion. I say this because I remain fair and objective and admit the European has introduced some positive achievements to the world. But it is super hard to applaud him when he has done so much dirt. The negative rings too loud. Each administration translates into murderers, butchers, sho'nuff invaders, and oppressors galore. Genuine human rights are outta here. A joke. Nostalgia at best. So consequently, we get "Wiki Leaks" and peers. With the advent of the internet and cell phones, that one move alone—little do mine know—has transformed the entire globe into a world of snitches. You read me right. A world of snitches. Can't fart lest the white man is there to smell it. So, should anyone try to connect the dots as to why I've engaged in some of the things that I have, and they may say one has nothing to do with the other. I happen to know and understand that I know what all of my sisters must be told, must come to learn, and must come to terms with: the brothers they are with now, in all probability, will not be with her 10 – 20 years from now because of the way society is set up. Mark my words, it does not satisfy me to merely narrate wrongs. Students of history recall how people used to tell Brother Frederick Douglass not to publish the names of his slave masters in his newspapers. But he wrote the slave masters' names, the names of the slaves they so-called owned, and, every now and then when the information reached him, he'd even publish the price paid for said slave.

To those who seek to unravel the many threads of history, do we not come upon irrefutable information with regard to the US going to war with Mexico alone and coming away with twice as much land? This "war" doubled the size of the United States. Expansionism??? Recall how, not quite 45 years ago, a TV commercial was run that said smoking was good for the human lungs? Today, in 2013, there are other commercials out on the topic of smoking cigarettes. Get this: Europeans have invented a "mechanical" cigarette. They also claim to have invented a pill to stop you from EVER getting gray hair. I read a report recently (March 2013) that, world-wide, hepatitis B has infected some 400 million people, and that of those, one million die from it each year. This is just one form of warfare being waged against us, dear people. The same report went on to say that a new disease is "discovered" and, sometimes, many per year. If we pay close attention, we'd see the African, Hispanic, Asian, and Indian are consistently "hit" by a "disease" of some sort.

Rev. Pat Robertson of the 700 Club stated on February 3, 2013, that there are over 300 million firearms in the hands of American people and that our food is more tainted today than ever before. I'm not partisan of the Bible—I'm strictly a realist. Point being, I recall reading in the Bible where it states: The harvest is plentiful, the workers are few. Do you get it, dear reader? Think about it for a spell, it'll come to you. The Bible also teaches that there is a time and a place for everything under the sun. Correct thinking has also suggested that man is to be pulled by logic and reason, not love and emotion. On September 11, 2011, PBS television reported $600 billion dollars had been spent on domestic security. I immediately commenced to entertaining the thought of what brought America to such a position. I flashed back to when I first read the work by Charles Darwin's *Origin of Species*. This was but 150 years ago when dear ol' Charles and his brother, Erasmus, may have fared far better if they would have concentrated on their very race itself.

It appears today that the entire world has taken up the position of leaving everything to the white race in terms of any and all problems. But again, if we would simply look and think, the churches of the Western folk have totally failed us. Notwithstanding, have you heard of any church scandals? Has the almighty white man stopped gun violence? Pregnant-at-an-early-age, babies-having-babies-ism? Tons of forms of abuse, neglect, homelessness in a land which boasts ever-so loudly about being the richest country that ever existed. Yet there's tent city dwelling over here.

Then there are the wars galore. America the harlot stays at war, always! When have ALL of America's troops ever been at home? When has this country not been at war? They have been at war with someone, somewhere, every day of their existence. So, with all this braggin' about how smart they are, perhaps not a matter of intelligence, but rather a lack thereof? Really now, stop and ponder these matters, for they are actually of life and death concern. As pragmatic as possible, I say maybe, just maybe, it's not so much about new evidence to convict this government, but a new way to look at old evidence. The white race is at war with the entire planet.

It is at odds with all forms of life, be that life in the form of a plant, liquid, oxygen... Their pipeline, stretching from as far as Canada to Arkansas, are to be held responsible for the biggest, most disastrous oil spills in the history of the earth. Check out what jumped in Kalamazoo, Michigan, the most expensive spill in history. Yet this country continues to increase risks to more bodies of water. Today, they move such dangerous materials by rail, truck, barge, or pipeline (as stated). Let us be clear: I am no scientist. I merely read all sorts of literature trying to keep myself abreast of what's jumping. This is certainly a form of warfare, like brother Marvin Gaye said in his song, "What's Going On." Say or make of it what you will, radiation and nuclear power are inherently unsafe. The price tag of industrial and social development has been unspeakable. Look at what has manifest since I've been captured and imprisoned. Coal miners trapped in the earth in staggering numbers. The spread of radiation via land-line, and now cell phones. The building and mass construction of what "they" call hydroelectric power dams. The mining and burning of coal. The destruction of the natural environment. Uni-Bomber and peers. Off-shore drilling and the innumerable deaths of nature's creatures, thanks to the Deep Water Horizon explosion and its massive oil spills.

The year 2010 was off the chart with disasters. Texas, Mexico, and the United Kingdom. Remember Three Mile Island in Pennsylvania in 1979, then the Soviet Union's Chernobyl in 1986? In Japan they witnessed Fukushima go up in March 2011 after a magnitude 9.0 earthquake, which is said to be to blame for a massive tsunami. An estimated 225,000 people died in Indonesia and Thailand after another earthquake followed by huge tsunamis. It's seldom talked about, but President Hugo Chavez of Venezuela spoke on how he had evidence that "Europeans" had developed weather warfare to the degree that they can now—through setting off explosives on the ocean floor—direct massive amounts of water (tsunamis) on to any land they so choose.

Remember now, Muslims have made this same accusation for the longest. Such leaders as Gaddafi and Saddam Hussein are now what? Dead as dead can get, and President Hugo Chavez as well. I'm confident you heard how he just, all of a sudden, became ill, tilted over, and died. Put your best foot forward connect the dots, and you will find that the Muslims have for the longest made accusations, especially of the Germans, of their inventing some new type of gun that looks like an umbrella and, when pointed at a human being, renders them unconscious immediately. Flash back to Brother Wayne Williams in Atlanta, all those little kids, brothers, and sisters came up missing. At least 15—I reiterate—while Brother Wayne Williams sat in a Georgia county jail awaiting trial. When Brother Dick Gregory and the Nation of Islam went on their fact finding mission, lo and behold, same accusations commenced to fly.

We must come to understand that there are a great many methods of war. It does not have to be bombs and bullets. Radiation is the new form of warfare. Contamination. Understand that contamination translates into future cancer casualties, and cases yet to manifest. Land lines, cell phones, computers, and all the other new "energy needs." Premature deaths and serious illnesses yearly around the globe reduces the population without firing a bullet. Imperialist property relations dominates the world and we know it not. We're out here chasing crack, tripping about where you were born, into so-called drive-bys, concerned about what Lebron and Ray Lewis gonna do next. Don't you think it might be a wise man's move to back-track and re-listen to the late, great, never-molested-a-child-in-his-life, Brother Michael Jackson's last cut, *Earth Song*? Yeah, what about that?

I decided to investigate what all the West has sallied forth, and the evidence is ultra-clear. Should you yourself launch an investigation, I'm sure you will discover the wanton disregard Capitalist have for the health and safety of people, especially workers and whoever else crosses their path. You shall also surely find that they could give less than a hussy-fuck about the long- and short-term consequences visited upon the natural environment. So yeah, like I said, ole Charlie Darwin should have spent his time tripping on his own plundering race. Me, I tend to put too much stock in the accusations brought forth by the late President Hugo Chavez with regard to weather warfare.

I can only hope that someday, somehow, some brother or sister may chance upon my words, views, and beliefs and conclude accurately. "Hey you know what? I read this book by a brother named Ashanti Ali. His book came up in our Black Student Union class. I don't think he was a quack, some psychopathic nut, or a serial killer. I seem to concur with those who say and feel he was naught but a revolutionary. Simple as that. He would kill a rock and put a brick in the hospital for his race. Especially sisters. The brother was alright. Perhaps a lil' extremist, but alright."

This is what I hope. If you know-it-all 'woods gonna label me, then do it correctly. Let this book reflect that I see myself as one practicing and promoting altruism in its rawest form. Yes, get to that!

I, Ashanti Ali, fully and completely agree with the Indians. These fork-tongued people are guilty of making war against the very planet itself. A super-sized plethora of evidence exists to substantiate a guilty verdict.

Dear reader, be happy, grateful and thankful for opportunities at your disposal. You can un-do wrongs committed by the enemy of all things.

Take firm steps to be a juggernaut and crush all wrongs and falsehoods as you encounter them. Unto the families of Brothers Emmitt Till, the Scottsboro Boys, Amadou Diallo, Oscar Grant, Rodney King, and our latest victimized families of Trayvon Martin and all the other people from our tribe who have experienced 100% racism and injustice, just know the following, and ponder these words if you would: That racist Zimmerman, who got away with murdering Trayvon, has actually served to shake and wake us from our 400 year slumber. Each and every time we undergo a loss, believe it or not, agree or disagree, we also obtain a victory. It will be slow in coming, but its arrival is as sure as there shall be more sunsets. A guarantee.

People in America feel they have a "right" to a home, a car, job, etc. No! That's not how it works. America wasn't founded for such. Likewise, think of these words as you will, America, but wasn't this country founded with the Black race being nothing but a "part" of it in mind? We were supposed to be slaves forever, but my fore parents had much to say about that. They used to hum:

"Gotta be strong, cuz there's so much to bear.
Gotta be courageous cuz there's so much to dare!"
"Nutthin changes if nutthin changes,
In good time, God rearranges."
"Listen to the clock as it tick and it tock,
Best believe,
The right combination opens the lock."

I am a soldier within the ranks of the Black Liberation Army. For one, I'm not trying to go back to Africa. I'm well aware it's my place of origin, however, my fight is right here under foot. To quote Brother Curtis Mayfield, "This is my country!" People harbor the opinion that going "back to Africa" will solve our problems, yet it is evident they don't see that by their doing so, leaving imperialism intact through our failure to dismantle and outright destroy, ensures they will regroup and visit our lands once again, wanting to borrow another cup of sugar. We all know what that led to, right?

To quote the late Amir Ak-Askari Ali (x-George Jackson), "I deny the existence of Black racism flat out by fiat. We have been placed in a unique and very dangerous environment, one which all races hate on us. I repeat, ALL. But some more than others. So consequently, we are in dire need of being re-educated a.s.a.p.! Keep uppermost the words of Emperor Haile Selassie, to study and examine all, but choose to follow only the good. What works, employ it."

Here in America, parents are held accountable for what their children do—or don't do—until they reach the age of 18. Properly translated, this axiomatically includes what our young learn—or don't learn. It is long past apparent that we have raised our youth up on an improper diet. Look at the outcome, people! Just look at it! Horrific. Yet we are still here. This translates as us being survivors. If nothing else, we must be bold for little Trayvon, Oscar, and the countless other brothers shot down and done away with by various means. We owe them that.

As for that racist, Zimmerman, why should we be surprised at what he did to young Trayvon? Likewise, we shouldn't be surprised by a jury's findings...that is, unless they find in our favor. And only then. At this juncture, July 2013, you mean to tell me Brother Malcolm X's words haven't reached you? Have you not reached a point as to where you can fully interpreciate what he was saying? You should start immediately to teach your young the *real* right from wrong; that we have been played, and in a major kinda way. That the sky will never open up to reveal some white man with a hellafied beard riding a chariot pulled by two horses—one having somehow grown the head of a dragon, and the other the head of a lion, and both having sprouted wings. And now, here comes our savior, floating through thin air after being dead for some two thousand years. As long as we allow lies such as that or those to be introduced unto our young, expect the worst. Expect to remain doormats. Expect to be beat and shot down at all times and places, with no respite or even semblance of justice.

Hold the elder generations accountable as they are to raise our young. Have you not become cognizant of the Nation of Islam's *Hate, That Hate Produced*? What ails you so much that you fail to properly educate your offspring, brothers? You are to protect our womenfolk and school your young, certainly not the other way around. Most certainly the sisters are not, that is, **not**, and I repeat for the third time, NOT, supposed to be found running a household without male support. That's not to say that a sister cannot do so—they have proven they can—but it's supposed to be a team effort, plain and simple. Moreover, just as we grew to a point that we could and did look at what our fathers and their fathers did, so will our young.

They shall come to know us as either soldiers, or cowards in the first degree. Contemplate, if you dare, on what you want written on your tombstone...

"I have died the ninth death of the cat,

Have seen Satan face to face, and turned my back

On God. Have dined in the swine's trough, and

Descended to the uttermost echelon of the pit.

Have entered the dew and seized my balls from the teeth of a roaring lion."

Eldridge Cleaver.

Aluta Continua!!

* President Hugo Chavez of Venezuela expired in March, 2013. He died mysteriously and suddenly. He was extremely outspoken, particularly of the United States government. He was looked upon by the U.S. government as an open enemy, and this is anything BUT a big Masonic Secret! Certainly we need many many more Hugo Chavezs! People who will call it like it is, regardless of the consequences.

* Be not surprised if North Korea all of a sudden experiences some phenomenon in the form of extreme weather damage, or the leader is suddenly struck down with a disease of some sort that ends his life. Also, keep an eye on the Republic of Iran. The U.S. has that country in its sights and plans to do away with it a.s.a.p.!

This is Ashanti. It is July 2013 in terms of the Western Roman calendar. Watch my words

Dedication

www.ingramcontent.com/pod-product-compliance
Lightning Source LLC
Chambersburg PA
CBHW030153100526
44592CB00009B/251